MONTLAKE LIBRARY
JAN 1 0 2017

NO LONGER PROPERTY OF
SEATTLE PUBLIC LIBRARY

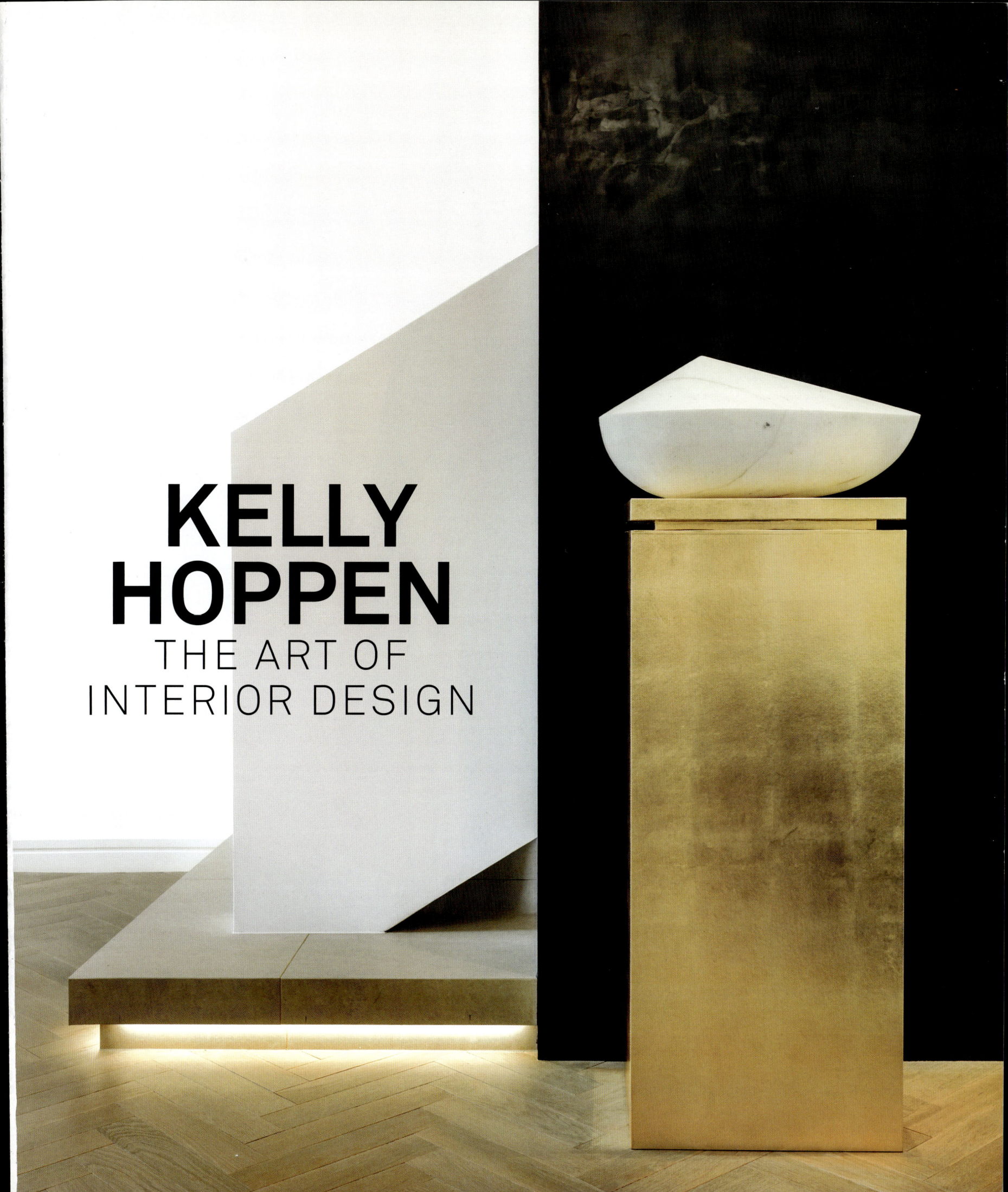

KELLY HOPPEN
THE ART OF INTERIOR DESIGN

HOPPEN

THE ART OF INTERIOR DESIGN

KELLY HOPPEN

For my mama, Stephanie, with all my love forever xxx

PAGE 1

A sculpture by Paul Vanstone sits on a plinth, covered with gold gilded wallpaper by de Gournay, in front of a runner of black specialist plaster that extends up the side of the staircase in my house.

LEFT

A collection of glass vessels is displayed in chrome-framed niches built into the white-lacquered timber cladding of a structural column.

OPPOSITE FROM TOP

The ribbed surface of a carved wooden artifact in contrast with the smooth curves of a glass fishbowl with a bouquet of cosmos. Chalky white ceramic vases and resin coral displayed on a Corian bathroom vanity unit in front of a wall clad in gray-veined Calacatta Oro marble. Three small ceramic bowls create an asymmetrical focus on one side of a traditional carved marble mantelpiece, with a runner of dramatic black polished plaster as the backdrop. A sandblasted opaque glass globe vase offsets the reflective surface of a polished nickel tray.

First published in the United States of America in 2016 by
Rizzoli International Publications, Inc.
300 Park Avenue South
New York, NY 10010
www.rizzoliusa.com

Originally published in the United Kingdom in 2016 by
Jacqui Small Llp
74–77 White Lion Street
London N1 9PF

Text copyright © Kelly Hoppen 2016

Text by Zia Mattocks

Text on pages 14, 27–31, 36, 46, 80, 92, 106, 128, 138, 150, 176, 202, 216, 224, 234, 243, 249, 268, 295, 310 copyright © Michelle Ogundehin 2016

Design and layout copyright © Jacqui Small 2016

Photography copyright © Jacqui Small Publishing, Mel Yates, Kelly Hoppen Interiors, Thomas Stewart, Bill Batten (and others—please see page 236)

Photography by Vincent Knapp, Mel Yates, Thomas Stewart, Bill Batten (and others—please see page 236)

The author's moral rights have been asserted.

All rights reserved. No part of this publication may be reproduced, stored in a retrieval system, or transmitted in any form or by any means, electronic, mechanical, photocopying, recording, or otherwise, without prior consent of the publishers.

2016 2017 2018 2019 / 10 9 8 7 6 5 4 3 2 1

ISBN: 978-0-8478-4894-2

Library of Congress Control Number: 2016941110

Printed in China

Publisher **Jacqui Small**
Senior Commissioning Editor **Eszter Karpati**
Managing Editor **Emma Heyworth-Dunn**
Writer and Project Editor **Zia Mattocks**
Editorial Assistant **Joe Hallsworth**
Designer **Robin Rout**
Production **Maeve Healy**

FOREWORD BY SIR TERENCE CONRAN   8
FORTY YEARS OF DESIGN   10
STRIKE A BALANCE   12
Q&A WITH MICHELLE OGUNDEHIN   26

TRADEMARKS   32
EAST MEETS WEST   34
GRID FLOW ZONE   44
UP & DOWN   78
MADE TO ORDER   90
SHINE   104
TRANSPARENT   126
TOUCH   136
STAY NEUTRAL   148

MOOD MAKERS   172
COLOR   174
SHED SOME LIGHT   200
ON REFLECTION   214
OBJECTS OF DESIRE   222

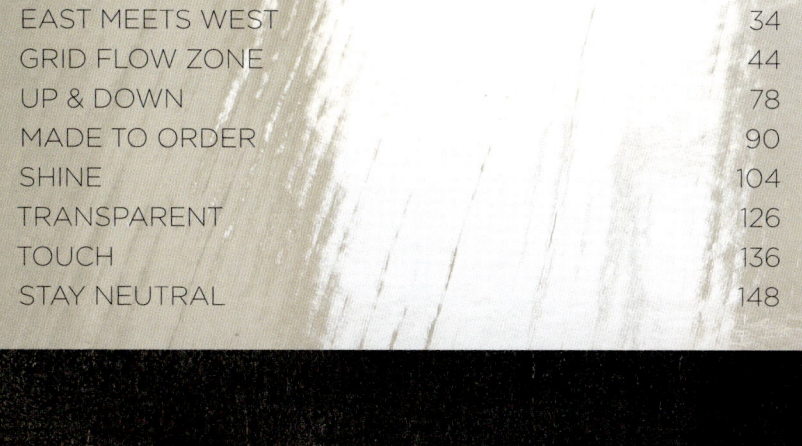

THE EDIT   240
MAKE AN ENTRANCE   242
LIVING SPACES   248
HEART OF THE HOME   268
BATHROOMS   294
SLEEP SANCTUARY   310

INDEX   324   ACKNOWLEDGMENTS   326

THIS PAGE

A stunning sculptural shelf, "Dune 01" (2007) by Zaha Hadid (Editions David Gill, London), floats on the wall like a pool of molten metal below an artwork by Nabil Nahas.

FOREWORD

BY SIR TERENCE CONRAN

This is a magnificent book, filled with the details that every designer should consider and which should stimulate their imagination so that they could try and do it better than Kelly—very unlikely. Her pages of imaginative details are superb; in fact, I find them more interesting than her full room sets toward the end.

I consider this book important as it clearly defines the difference between a designer and a decorator. The latter usually only takes responsibility for the color of the walls and the carpet or rug, the sofa and its upholstery fabric, a light fixture or two, and a bowl of flowers; whereas, if you look at the detail that Kelly has so admirably demonstrated, it shows the thought a true designer puts into their projects. I also find it interesting that she considers the mood of a room—a great idea.

I would also like to compliment Kelly's clients for having funded this very profound detail, which I find quite exquisite. Every designer should study this book carefully before they begin their next project. I will!

Terence

FORTY YEARS OF DESIGN

Forty years! It's hard to believe, as every day has been a joy and never felt like work. My passion and love for design have driven me in such an incredible way that it was only when beginning to write my "retrospective" book that the magnitude of what I was about to begin dawned on me.

It has been such a cathartic year, choosing and compiling the images I wanted to use—from such a vast archive—and including new work, literally hot off the press. When I started to look through the images of my past work, I had such vivid memories of every single project that it felt as though it was only yesterday when I had handed them over to my clients.

I have been wonderfully lucky to work with some incredible people, in amazing countries all over the world. I believe my philosophy and design ethos, and what the process means to me, have allowed me to design for like-minded people, and I feel honored.

My dream was, and still is, to create homes for people to live in, and, foremost, to make people feel as though they have lived in them all their lives, but with the added bonus of the excitement of the new. The smell of fresh paint and the newness of objects—as well as the familiarity of the old, placed into a space like art: that is the excitement for me, just making it all come together. For me, designing is like cooking a recipe and adding all the herbs and spices to create the best taste you can imagine.

My book, *The Art of Interior Design*, is a mixture of old and new, of forty years of work, and I hope you enjoy reading and looking through it as much as I have enjoyed creating it.

I have always said, "If I can dream it, I can design it."

Thank you,

Love, Kelly

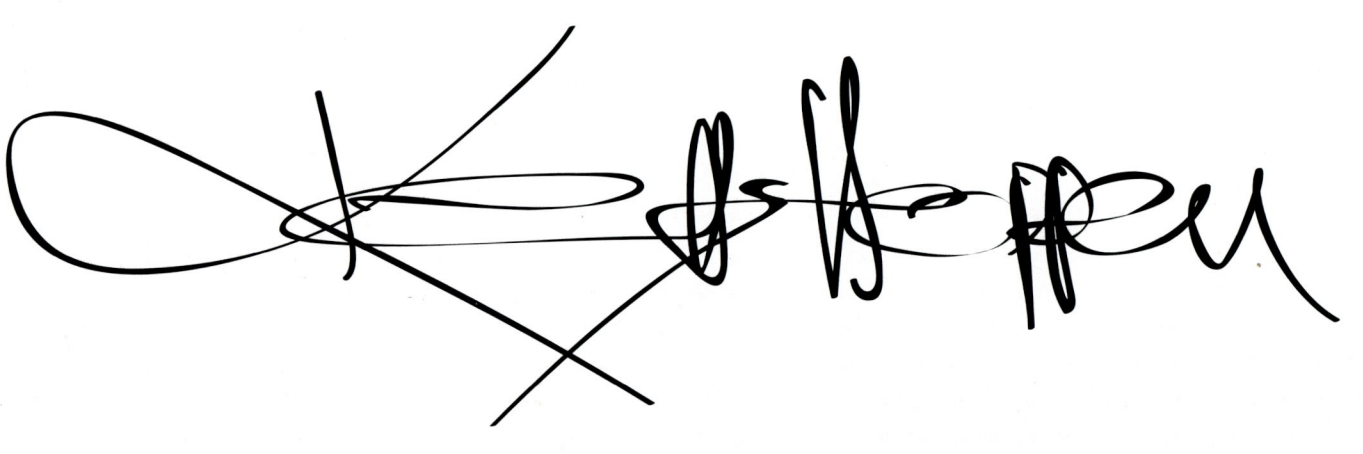

STRIKE

STRIKE A BALANCE

The Kelly Hoppen brand has always been about the best quality. But the core value, for me, is to create homes for people to live in. It isn't about them looking immaculate and perfect—in fact, I've struggled with that in my own mind—it's about creating spaces you can breathe in. It's a purist style, with tactile materials, furnishings, and objects, because, above all, a house has to feel right.

It's also about the number, combination, and placement of things: balance. It's about where you put things and where you don't. It's knowing where a picture should be on a wall—how high or low, or how many. Just as in calligraphy, where it's not the letters themselves but the space around them that's really important, it's often what you don't put in a space that matters the most. And the beauty of home is that by changing just one thing, you can make it all new.

Your eye will always be drawn to the things you love, and if your home can make you happy from what you have inside it, well, that is success. But not everyone knows how to achieve that goal, so this is where I come in. I think home should be a place that your kids can keep coming back to, a place that's safe. My job is to create that sort of safeness. That's one of my talents. That's what I love.

PREVIOUS PAGE

A stunning centerpiece has been created in this dressing area by hanging a magnificent stainless-steel chandelier from Hudson low over a Robert Kuo table with a sculptural tree-trunk base of antique copper. The strands of chainmail pool on the white-lacquered tabletop, where a collection of silver bowls and vases is displayed. A mirror opposite the window reflects light and creates balance, as does the symmetry of the framed photographs on either side of the bedroom door.

OPPOSITE

Striking a balance also depends on introducing a note of asymmetry. This is the first view I see as I walk through my front door. My entrance hall is designed on the grid, with striking concentric frames of black-and-white marble on the floor. The centerpiece is the custom-made lacquer-topped table I designed with its sculptured bronze base made by Matt Stanwix. Hanging directly above this is a trio of bespoke pendant lights by Hervé Langlais for Galerie Negropontes, beyond which my portrait of Marilyn Monroe can be admired. Another black-and-white photograph hangs on the opposite wall, while the Japanese-style runner of taupe wood, which here conceals a closet, is repeated to the right of the front door, creating a balanced but asymmetrical effect.

COUNTDOWN IMAGES ON FOLLOWING PAGES

10 A simple line of black tea caddies makes an understated and unusual display on a traditional marble mantelpiece, with an off-center picture breaking up the strict symmetry.
9 Everyday objects are given importance by repetition. Here, a grid formation of moss balls in cylindrical glasses has a graphic impact on a mirror-and-lacquer Kelly Hoppen coffee table.
8 Locally sourced Panama hats make an apt display on the wall of a Barbados beach house.
7 The soft gray of the porcelain figurines of Oriental soldiers tones with the plaster wall behind. The change in height creates interest.
6 Azadeh Shladovsky's organic cubes of dark oak with matte brass inlays can be used individually as stools or side tables; pushed together, as here, they make a stunning alternative coffee table.
5 The curved backs of Hans Wegner's Wishbone chairs contrast with the straight edge of the table.
4 Domes of synthetic grass look like art on a white gravel and black stone rooftop terrace.
3 Light filters through linen mesh curtains onto a row of handmade black-lacquered resin jars.
2 Pieces of resin coral, encased in glass on black oak recessed ledges, are elevated to artworks.
1 A perfect stone globe plays against the hard lines and matte and glossy surfaces of a garden.

10

7

5

4

2

I have been interviewed many times over the course of my career and it is always interesting to see how a Q&A session develops. Some questions are predictable but others lead the conversation in unexpected and fascinating directions. As Editor in Chief of *Elle Decoration* UK, the leading magazine on contemporary design and interiors, there is no one more appropriate to interview me for my retrospective book than Michelle Ogundehin.

I've read that when you were a child, you loved to play with pop-up books, the kind that open up like a 3-D world. It strikes me that this is all about stage-setting, which is a lot of what home-making is too. How early on did you realize that your life path had to be design and interiors?

KH Very early. My mother said that at thirteen years old I was in the bathroom laying out my bottles and making everything beautiful. But I was obsessed with those pop-up books from much younger. I'd play with them for hours, creating stories in my mind—I always wanted to get into the back of them. I was really into the structure of how things worked. I'd even cut out pieces and move them around inside.

But a pivotal moment for me was when I was about 11. I was allowed to redecorate my childhood bedroom, which was *very* pink. My mother said I could change it if I knew what I wanted, which I absolutely did. Firstly, I wanted to swap rooms with my brother because he was at boarding school, so that was agreed, and then I asked for cream shag-pile carpet, chocolate-brown felt trimmed with chrome for the walls, white shutters on all the closets, and an incredible silver Robin Day chair with holes in it that I'd seen; my brother still has it in his studio today. The only doubtful thing was the comforter, which was brown and white. I wanted this sort of modern pop-art bedroom.

What about your parents? Were they into design and interiors? I'm intrigued to understand whether your talent is innate, inherited, or learned?

KH When I was growing up I was surrounded by this very bohemian London lifestyle, with my mother and all her literary and artist and sculptor friends, and my father's fashion business. And because I was living at home, I was very much included in it, always at dinners, listening to people, soaking it all up like a sponge. But my mother's style was incredibly varied. Her study was amazing, all metal and smoked brown glass from Ciancimino. The dining room was not my thing, very green and white with trellis, like the inside of a conservatory, but still stylish, as was my parents' bedroom. It had a low bed covered with zebra fabric, with low side tables—very modern and cool—and then her living room was very traditional with an amazing collection of glass bells. I think her style was very diverse, which was great for me because I was exposed to all these different looks and she loved it, and it was warm and inviting.

I was very house-proud, though, and my mom was quite messy, which she'll hate me for saying but it's true. She'd go out and I'd somehow convince the au pair to help me move furniture across the room. When other kids were watching TV shows, I was moving furniture around. On weekends, my mom would ask me what I wanted to do, and I'd say I wanted to go and look at show homes. In those days they were really prevalent, and they'd always have open days. My mum loved interiors and art, so we'd have great fun together. We'd go to museums and art galleries all the time, too, so from a very early age my childhood was incredibly informative in the arts.

I also had a great aunt, who lived in a beautiful six-story house one street away from us. Most days after school I'd go and see her. She had this incredible study with love seats upholstered in bright orange velvet, an amazing Amtico floor that looked like marble with brass inlays, and a pair of drinks cabinets with mirrored glass so they looked like they went on forever. We used to sit down and just talk about her house and life—she was a larger-than-life character with amazing taste and a phenomenal air. I was obsessed with her style.

So that's where my love for home came in. I was very fortunate to be able to go into homes like that, and those of my mother's extraordinary mix of friends. But it came entirely from me; nobody said, "Go and do interiors."

Digging a little deeper, you were born in South Africa, so I'm wondering what influence this heritage might also have had on you? I know you left when you were two, but you've often spoken very warmly of returning every Christmas to visit your grandmother. Do these memories continue to inform you today?

> "My style evolved in a very organic way—it was real and intuitive."

KH My father, who is British, took the *QE2* over to South Africa for work, and he met my South African mother, who lived in Constantia, just south of Cape Town. Her family home was incredible; without a doubt, it partly made me who I am. I have a memory of every part of that house. It was extraordinary, with loads of antiques, incredible fabrics, and wonderful art. My grandmother's china cabinets were full of Venetian glass and accessories that we'd use to set the table every Friday night. I'd go out into her hydrangea garden, famous in Cape Town, to cut flowers for the table, too. I'd bake heart-shaped chocolate cakes in the kitchen with Ella, my grandmother's cook. Upstairs I'd crochet, and we'd look out of the windows at night to see whether the gorillas would come and shake the plum trees. I used to get into bed with my grandmother every morning and we'd have boiled eggs and homemade soda-bread soldiers with Marmite and cottage cheese and a cup of tea. I even still remember the smell of my grandfather's aftershave, the way he'd put his watch on, and these incredible silk shirts he'd had made in Europe. I loved that I always went back and nothing had changed. It was all part of an amazing time spent with cousins, aunts, and uncles. And, I suppose, because I had tragedy later in life, with my parents divorcing and then my father dying when I was still so young, this was a crucial—and genuinely happy—time for me.

For you to be celebrating 40 years of practice, you must have started work incredibly young, and with no time for any formal training?

KH Yes! I got my first project through my stepfather when I was sixteen-and-a-half. He had a friend who wanted a kitchen done. It was in Elvaston Place in London. He was an alcoholic, but somehow we managed to get some builders through him, who were the same. It was a disaster! I mean, it was hideous, but what mattered was I made a job happen. And then the next project came a year later, through a girlfriend of mine who knew Guy Edwards, the Grand Prix racing driver. He asked me to decorate his massive house in The Boltons, and that was basically the beginning of my career. I was very lucky to be given the chance based on my own apartment that he had seen.

And you had no doubts? Surely you were scared? It seems an incredibly audacious thing to be decorating people's homes as a teenager?

KH I was just so happy to be out of school, and so happy to be in control. By the age of seventeen I'd bought and done up my own apartment in Chelsea and set up an office there. The kitchen was pretty awful—I painted it peacock blue—but the living room and the bedroom were good. I remember, I'd bought this Chinese lacquered trunk at Portobello, too, so my love of East meets West was already starting. And I had my first proper studio, on 134 Lots Road, about two years later.

I was lucky. I did a fantastic job for Guy Edwards and from that I got another racing driver, Keke Rosberg, just before he won the World Championship, and then a couple of actors, including Martin Shaw. I remember it was a very exciting time at the beginning, and from there is history and discretion.

But I feel so fortunate to have been so young when I started this process. Back then, everything came from a real intrigue and experience, rather than what I feel people do today, which is just to open up a book and copy from it. My style evolved in a very organic way—it was real and intuitive. I was developing my thing and building my team. Also, since I was a little girl, I'd traveled during every school vacation, seeing old buildings, art, and museums all over Europe, then every year going back to South Africa, and always going to art galleries, so I had this very different, international perspective. And then, of course, my love for the East became an obsession.

You have to remember that in those days there wasn't the Internet, it was about word of mouth and physically trawling the design centers and shops. For example, I discovered this man on Great Portland Street who sold calico, burlap, and mattress ticking, and, because I couldn't afford expensive materials, I'd use these as the main fabrics instead. So when I was doing up some of the houses, I'd use calico and ticking to upholster the chairs and add some stitching, but then throw in lacquer or a delicate Fortuny pillow, and that was what made this eclectic look that started a trend.

You have the most incredible recall for detail. And when you design, you've often said it comes straight from the heart, that you have a very intuitive way of working, distilling everything you've seen, heard, smelt, and felt into a singular and tangible vision. How does this work?

KH The interesting thing is I'm very dyslexic, but I only found out when my daughter Natasha was diagnosed. I couldn't read out loud at school. I couldn't copy anything; the spelling would be wrong, even if I tried as hard as I could. However, if you showed me a page with lots of pictures on it and I looked at it for ten or fifteen minutes, I would have memorized it. So, visually, my IQ is way off the charts, but writing and reading are impossible. My brain just works in a different way.

For example, I can walk into a room and scan it in five minutes and know what to do to make it better. I see a blank canvas and lines start to appear. And as I'm describing it, I can literally *see* it. So when I'm designing, I can physically visualize a space in 3-D before it's built. I can take things out and move them around in my mind's eye, too. I think this really helps me because I'm never jailed by the floor plan. I start with no assumptions of what can and can't be done. I'll make the space work for me. Whereas if you go in with restrictions from day one, you'll never really stretch your imagination, and my imagination is the greatest gift I've ever been given.

We often talk about the best and most successful homes being someone's personally curated corner of the world, their home as their life, and the idea that a space like that is created slowly over years, and yet your role is to effectively craft this feeling more immediately. How is this possible?

KH It's lots of different layers. You meet someone and they're always going to be nervous, but I'm just excited about embarking on a new project. Then they start talking and the more they say, the more they start to relax and we start to engage, and that's the beginning of building a relationship. It's just like at a dinner party, discovering what you have in common with someone else.

> "If *was* influenced by trends, I don't think I would have lasted so long."

And after we've pinned down the fundamentals, what I call the basic wardrobe of the home—the floors, walls, and hard finishes—and the feel, I start to show people samples, furniture, lighting, and so on that I think they might like, based on what they've said. It's about delving further into that person's mind, their relationship with their partner, spouse, children, and how they work as a team, in order to create the personal space.

When you build a home for someone, some don't really know what they want; all they *can* know is how they want to feel in it. For me, it's a process of understanding that. It's an art and it doesn't happen immediately. It's hard. Getting into someone's head is intriguing and brilliant, and I love that part. That, for me, is what good design is all about. You have to keep digging away to get the words, and then the words have to be attached to something that's tangible. And you have to be completely selfless, so you can guide someone with style to fulfill *their* dream. When I first started, I definitely had more of an ego. I wanted to impose what *I* thought was best, but now the process is much more organic and second nature—with no ego! What I won't let go of, though, is making everything stylish and beautiful.

How have you navigated the evolution of taste over the years since you started, from the vagaries of showpiece homes and extravagantly swagged window treatments in the early 1980s, via the pure minimalist look, to current ideas of home as a cocoon of security and warmth?

KH The thing is, I don't take notice of trends. It's weird. Maybe it's because I'm so busy and always in my own head, but my influences come from things like art, fashion, vintage, music, people, and conversation. I tend to look at trends and where things are going a bit like fashion—it's there and it's not, and it's not substantial enough to make it important to me. I remember when minimalism came in, though. I steered very far away from it because it didn't feel like me, and when people called me a minimalist, it would drive me mad. I consider myself a purist. John Pawson is the greatest minimalist of all time, and what he does is incredible, but I wouldn't know how to do it. It wouldn't be natural to me, and I wouldn't enjoy it. I know what I love and what excites me about design, and I can design so quickly when it's true to me. If I *was* influenced by trends, I don't think I would have lasted so long.

So where do you get your inspiration from? I know your style is based on several core seams of influence, from the organic world to Eastern influences, but what fires your imagination on a daily basis?

KH My brain is continually collating bits of information from everywhere. I always get inspired by things that have nothing to do with design. I'll give you an example: in Ibiza one year, I'd been on vacation for nearly a month, which is very unusual for me, and as it came toward the end of the vacation, I drove past this typically Ibizan house with a run of ocher yellow down the side and I remember consciously thinking, I've got to clock that because it gives me an idea for a job that I'm doing. And then suddenly, boom! It was the moment I came out of vacation mode and all the things that I'd seen in the last three-and-a-half weeks started filtering back into the virtual filing system in my head. It was when I realized that I needed downtime to restock my brain in order to be able to use it.

There are certain places that have influenced me, too, like Paris, but it's the essence of the city, rather than a specific detail—the feeling of the place, the flea markets, the way Parisians dress, the flirtation, their use of unexpected pieces and the juxtaposition of fabrics—that *je ne sais quoi*. I know a lot of people find Swedish and Danish design very inspiring, but that was never me. Italy, though, is a big influence. The Italians have a way of putting things together that on paper really shouldn't work, but they pull it off. And New York: it's the fast pace, and the way they live. I like scale, I'm never frightened of it, even in small buildings. New York is very inspiring in every way.

Vintage furniture, too, is inspirational. I think you can create a whole room around a piece, rather than the other way around. I also have a lot of photographs, and a box of tearsheets that I've kept for years in my studio. And collections of things: a belt buckle I loved, a picture of bare flesh against silk sheets. I just keep logging those references in the basement of my brain, which is huge. I don't think I ever discard anything, so I can just pull things back up. And when my head gets full, I go away again for a week.

You've said that the art of design is about using space, light, and texture to engender good feelings. Do you think that a well-designed space can actually be beneficial for your well-being, or even improve your health?

KH Absolutely, 100 percent. I've been into homes that were dark and felt wrong in every way, so much so that I needed to get out, so if you lived in a space like that, it's surely going to have an effect on you. But today anybody can paint their walls white and make it look brighter. It's just not necessary to live in spaces that don't feel right. No matter what budget you're on, you can brighten up your home. I'd like to think that I can make people happier in their environments, and hopefully from that, if they had some sort of ailment, they might begin to heal. After all, being positive about yourself in mind, body, and spirit can definitely make you healthier. What you eat makes you healthier, so what you look at, what you touch, your environment, the music you listen to have all got to have an effect.

And finally, after 40 years, how do you feel about beige and taupe? Are you still in love with neutrals?

KH Looking through this book, you can see that I *do* use color but it's more accents of color. I like the way a neutral room feels and then the way a color will sharpen it. But if we think of some of the greats, like David Hicks (his book on interiors was the first one I bought), he was a genius at pattern, and I couldn't do that. The great traditionalists, like John Stefanidis, they owned their style. Terence Conran—you *know* who he is: a genius. Philippe Starck, Kelly Wearstler, whether you like it or not, they *own* their style. That's what I admire. So I'm not frightened of using color but neutrals are who I am. It's worked for 40 years— it was needed—and I'll continue in the "Hoppen" style.

TRADE

MARKS

EAST MEETS WEST

*This is a truly modern style
that runs like a thread through all my work*

TRADEMARKS

Asian cultures are still the biggest influence on me; it's a theme that comes back again and again in my work because the Eastern notions of tranquility and subtle texture ring very true in my heart, and they have done so right from the beginning of my career. And although such philosophies of design can also be quite rigid and formulated, they come from the point of view that simplicity and order create calmness and harmony; and that alignment, rows of things, and repetition all enhance balance, and I love that. But the way I use these influences works because it's always just a taste of the East, and this, mixed with contemporary Western design, makes my style decidedly modern. This is what creates homes that are clean-lined and contemporary, simple yet exotic.

PREVIOUS PAGE

Tantalizingly glimpsed through Eastern-style black linen panels, the bed in this perfectly balanced composition has been dressed with a sensuous mix of fabrics that soften its concrete base and create a warm mood: off-white ostrich leather for the padded headboard, mouse-gray satin for the eiderdown, charcoal flannel for the stacked pillows, and red velvet for the runner. It is this flash of rich color that draws the eye.

OPPOSITE

Contrasts of texture, shape, and proportion are achieved in this simple but effective display of three miniature glass-encased moss balls, placed centrally on three shiny black-lacquered Flibuste tables by Christian Liaigre. The round shapes contrast with the ridges of the rug, which is reminiscent of the raked gravel in a Zen garden.

TRADEMARKS

FUSION

THIS PAGE AND OPPOSITE

There is beauty in simplicity. All these interior details perfectly illustrate how an understated but texturally rich neutral color scheme, with natural woods and linens, and accents of black or charcoal, allows the Eastern elements to sing. Items such as a bronze Buddha, lacquered boxes, scrolls decorated with calligraphy, and simple ceramics all strike the right note in a home decorated with a fusion of Eastern and Western styles.

EAST MEETS WEST

By designing instinctively, as I do, interpreting my clients' wants and needs for their home, I have found that blending Eastern elements and design principles into Western interiors is a seamless process that results in the most balanced, elegant homes that are easy to live in and that suit our modern way of life. A comfortable, inviting home should be both contemporary and flexible, functional, fit for purpose, and serving the needs of all who live there, but with touches of originality and style that make it truly personal and a joy to be in.

As a very visual person, I am constantly inspired by all that is around me—fashion, art, landscapes, buildings, objects, people, and the natural world. That spark of creativity never stops and it is what drives me to keep designing and evolving my style. Influences from other cultures have always played a big part in this, particularly those of Southeast Asia, China, and Japan, but also Africa, India, and Europe.

The objects and treasures you bring into your home reveal a lot about your personality and, whatever their origins, the important thing is that they connect with your sensibilities and resonate with each other. A neutral color scheme makes a restrained backdrop for an eclectic interior, as it won't fight for attention but offers quiet layers of interest and texture to offset displays, art, and star pieces. One of the things I love most about Eastern design is the respect for natural materials and traditional skills and craftsmanship, so East-meets-West interiors will invariably feature natural or stained wood, stone, bronze, lacquer, natural matting, and linen.

TRADITION

Eastern interiors are typically designed to create an optimum balance of opposites—yin and yang, feminine and masculine, dark and light, coolness and warmth, curved and straight. Value is placed on humble materials and beauty is found in everyday items. The use of color tends to be clean, assured, and graphic. Carefully considered splashes of rich, deep, or bright colors are introduced to neutral or monochrome palettes to add bold contrast and arrest the attention. Typically lacquer-red, burnt orange, saffron, magenta, indigo, or emerald are tempered with shades of white, cream, or black to outline and define. As with other aspects of Eastern design, restraint is the order of the day; a subtle injection of one or two bold hues has the greatest impact. The textures and finishes of the various elements have a great impact on the mood of a space. Many jewel-like hues shine brightest in rich textures, such as glossy lacquer, deep-pile velvet, heavy raw silk, or ornate brocade, which all engender an opulent feel. Play with contrasts: think of the effect of a rough-weave rug layered on polished dark floorboards, a shiny lacquer box on a rustic wood table, a mother-of-pearl button on a cashmere pillow, or a silk trim on a linen drape.

Inspiration for decorative schemes can be found in all things, from the view of a landscape that provides the basis for a color palette, to the sash on a traditional Japanese kimono that is reinterpreted as a silk pillow band, to the carved paneling in an Indonesian temple that becomes the basis for a screen in an open-plan space. With the unifying force of the Internet, as well as the ease of global travel and trade, the cross-fertilization between cultures has never been so pronounced nor have these influences been more instantly accessible; they are, quite literally, at our fingertips.

OPPOSITE

A cozy seating area is made warm and inviting by the traditional color combination of mellow, earthy shades of terracotta offset by cream, black, neutral tones, and natural wood. The divan upholstered in striped linen fabric is piled high with pillows in true East-meets-West style.

ABOVE RIGHT AND RIGHT

Simple objects can be elevated to greater importance when grouped together in an interesting way. Humble white pots, arranged asymmetrically to arrest the eye, stand out beautifully against the dark wood of this display cabinet and contrast dramatically with the opulent gold dragon, while the open door of an antique cabinet reveals an intriguing collection of Oriental scrolls.

TRADEMARKS

SIMPLICITY

It is not only how things look that strike a chord with me but also how they make me feel, and it is perhaps the calm, harmonious qualities of the Eastern aesthetic that speak the loudest to me. As the pace of modern life and, along with it, the accumulation of material possessions seem to accelerate at an alarming rate, the Eastern love for simplicity and order is easy to relate to. We are constantly advised that decluttering our homes and workspaces of unnecessary items will lead to a clearer mind and a calmer mood, where we can relax, breathe, identify our priorities, and work out what makes us truly happy and fulfilled. When I design, I always follow the principles of feng shui, the ancient Chinese art that ensures the free flow of energy within a space and harmonizes it in order to optimize the health and good fortune of its inhabitants.

A tranquil home is a joy to return to after the demands of the day—a peaceful haven filled with objects, art, music, and scent that lift the spirit and feed the soul. A light, airy, uncluttered interior with a thread of continuity throughout also maximizes the sense of space in homes that are not as generously sized as we would like. Having fewer objects and multipurpose furniture lets you appreciate architectural details and brings the qualities of materials, design, and workmanship to the fore. With its pared-back simplicity, clean lines, and neutral tones, combined with rich textural contrasts, touches of glamour, and confident injections of color and individuality, East meets West is a style that has underpinned my work ever since I began designing interiors.

ABOVE RIGHT

Rectangular panels of sandblasted glass echo the geometric wall decoration and contrast with the curved lamp stand. The panels are reminiscent of a Japanese rice-paper screen and create interesting effects of transparency and opacity without blocking the light.

RIGHT

This wide pivoting door opens to offer a view into the space beyond, also decorated in off-white tones. Continuity is further achieved by the symmetrical repetition of the pairs of narrow windows, which tie in with the long, thin door handles and together emphasize the vertical grid.

OPPOSITE

The mezzanine area above the double door makes the most of the space and houses two large storage baskets. Materials and colors are kept neutral, with the only decoration being the two vertical banners of calico and scrim, which emphasize the doorway, and the moss balls on the stairs, echoed by the plants on the windowsill in the room beyond.

GRID

These principles

FLOW

are the foundations

ZONE

of all my designs

TRADEMARKS

There are certain places where you have to go into a room and shake hands with it first. You have to form a relationship with the space before you can start to design it. It's about understanding it, so that you can begin to shape it. And the way I design on a grid is the basis of that. I see a blank canvas, and lines start to appear. These lines all work together, framing views and creating harmonious connections between the different planes of a room, from the walls, floors, and doors to the way the space links to other rooms or zones. It's about flow, for the eye as well as for the overall balance of the space. And because the grid is the bone structure of a room, designing on a grid ensures there is a fluid conversation between all the different components, which in turn underpins how that space will feel.

PREVIOUS PAGE

The horizontal and vertical lines in this dramatic entrance lobby are clearly defined. Slatted and cleverly lit dark timber walls arch above the polished marble runner set into the wooden floor and, together with the suspended lanterns by Kevin Reilly, draw the eye onward.

OPPOSITE

In this Manhattan apartment, the grid has been used in a practical way, with the sliding, slatted-paneled shoji screen separating the living and dining spaces as well as emphasizing the vertical lines of the room. The square shape and clean lines of the Christian Liaigre sofa, ottoman, coffee table, and pair of floor lamps are balanced by the curves of the bowls, table lamp, and Robert Kuo side table. The effect is very Japanese in style.

OVERLEAF

This image perfectly illustrates how every element within the open-plan dining space and seating area in my London home has been chosen to emphasize the grid, from the structural pillars and beams to the steps and shelf, to the drapes, lights, furniture, and even the line of pots in the center of the tabletop.

TRADEMARKS

STRUCTURE

The grid defines the lines of a room, forming a framework of verticals and horizontals—the structural "bones"—against which various elements can be aligned. It is the foundation of any design, allowing you to determine where the focus of the room should be and whether you need to correct its proportions or accentuate architectural features within it.

ABOVE

To enclose the dining space within this compact open-plan living area, I designed a "cage" of black timber beams, running across the ceiling and down to the floor. The structure makes a strong grid statement and creates a feeling of containment while retaining an open feel. Note the matte texture that plays against the glossy bespoke table and marble floor.

OPPOSITE

A detail of the shoji screens shown on page 47, seen here from the dining area. When closed, the slatted blackened oak forms a wall of texture.

For example, deeper and more pronounced baseboards, chair rails, picture rails, and floating shelves will make a room seem wider and longer, whereas vertical panels, pillars, tall cabinetry, or full-length drapes will make the ceiling seem higher. If everything is chosen and positioned with the grid in mind, nothing will be out of place.

THIS PAGE AND OPPOSITE

For monochromatic schemes, dark stained wood is the only option and the dramatic contrast between the black joinery and the white walls is eternally chic. All these images illustrate how joinery can be used to emphasize the grid, from the black picture frame and clothes rails (right), to the windowpane grid along one side of a corridor echoed by the row of pictures by Judith K McMillan on the facing wall (opposite below right), to the floor-to-ceiling sliding doors in a bathroom (opposite above right), and the two examples of concealed storage in custom-made dressing rooms: louvered doors (opposite below left) and grooved timber, lit up to highlight their contours and the bust by Ralph Brown (opposite above left). The leather border on the pale silk carpet is another way of defining the grid, drawing the eye forward and accentuating the length of the room.

Assessing a space and planning the layout is something that has always come naturally to me because I find it very easy to visualize a room in three dimensions—a cuboid made up of six vertical and horizontal planes: four walls, a ceiling, and a floor. How you divide up the space and, ultimately, how it is decorated, furnished, and lit, all depend on the principles of the grid system, successful zoning, and creating a good flow throughout.

Commissioning bespoke joinery is a great way to exploit the potential of the grid within a room, as it makes a strong impact and can be used to emphasize either vertical or horizontal lines, depending on the design. Custom-made cabinetry is a practical solution for housing all manner of objects, books, media equipment, clothes, and shoes—with the options of open shelving or cubbyholes for displays, floor-to-ceiling doors to keep everything hidden away, or sliding panels that partially reveal the contents. Joinery forms an important part of the room's internal architecture and makes a dominant decorative statement, so the choice of material and finish needs careful consideration.

OPPOSITE

This dramatic corridor—a cocoon of marble and mirror—is all about the grid, starting with the black marble floor inset with "frames" of white marble. The deep-grooved, dark wood wall panels and ceiling coffers are cleverly lit to enhance the effect, with the additional patterns created by the two-tone brass pendants by CTO Lighting. Their design reflects the sculpture on the plinth, which is the focal point that draws the eye, while the mirror-clad end wall creates a sense of infinity.

ABOVE LEFT

A detail of the wooden beam structure that defines the dining zone seen on page 50, with a built-in bench seat emphasizing the horizontal lines of the grid. The reflections in the panels of mirror in between the vertical beams make the space seem larger and brighter.

ABOVE RIGHT

The view of the living area from the custom-made desk of black and white lacquer with brass inlays—the focal point of the study—is framed by the open sliding doors of smoked glass with a polished brass trim. Runners of dark timber slats extend up the wall behind the desk and onto the ceiling, defining the grid, leading the eye onward, and uniting the two spaces.

LEFT

An upholstered, metal-framed 1960s chair is beautifully showcased against the backdrop of sliding closet doors, almost elevating it into a piece of sculpture. The light filtering through the open shutters highlights the grain of the dark wood and the grooved central panels. These custom-made, dressing-room-style closets ran along one entire wall of my bedroom in a previously owned house.

Once I have explained the concept of the grid and how it works by providing the framework that informs and underpins every other design decision, people are quick to recognize the horizontal and vertical elements in rooms where I have used dark wood or panels of boldly contrasting materials to emphasize them. In more muted tone-on-tone schemes, however, the grid may not be so immediately obvious but it is still very much at play in my designs, giving spaces quiet strength and subtle definition through changes of texture and finish. The overall effect is calm and tranquil but perfectly balanced.

THIS PAGE AND OPPOSITE

Two views of the main sitting area within the vast open-plan first floor of my home, a former auction house in central London, decorated in calm shades of taupe and white (opposite and above left). I bought the building as a shell, with nothing but a floor, an impressively high ceiling, and the structural columns. I clad the columns in pale wood panels inset with horizontal runners of nickel and bronze (above and below right). These create frames within the space, defining the three-dimensional grid, together with the amazing floor-to-ceiling slatted doors, reminiscent of Japanese shoji screens. The linear sofa and marble shelf define the horizontal lines of the room, while low-hanging pendant lights, with their oversized glass bubbles blown by DARK that do not interrupt the views from any angle, bring the focus to mid-level.

RUNNERS

Also sometimes called "banners," runners are bands of a contrasting material or color that run through floors, up walls, over tabletops, sofas, and beds, and around pillows. As well as giving the room definition by underlining the grid structure, runners provide an effective way to connect various elements of the space together or to forge visual links by repeating a color, texture, or material that has been used elsewhere within the scheme in another context.

CLOCKWISE FROM LEFT

Runners can take many forms: a dividing wall of slatted dark wood at Rhodes W1 restaurant; a stunning double-aspect fireplace that emphasizes the horizontal lines within both a hallway and a living room; a narrow polished stainless-steel runner contrasting with the warm tones of the wooden floor, while dark wood runners give structure to the padded linen walls of a yacht; a dark, rough-textured runner within a pale painted wall, defining the fireplace in a monochromatic living room; reminiscent of a necklace, nickel upholstery tacks decorating the seam in this ALMA leather floor in jewelry designer Stephen Webster's flagship store; a dramatic dark wood runner slicing through the taupe tiled wall, giving the raised bathtub a real presence.

GRID, FLOW, ZONE

Runners can range from the narrowest strips to very wide bands; they may be soft or hard, in contrasting colors or tone on tone. For example, a marble runner within a wooden floor could form a "pathway" through a hall and into a living space, perhaps continuing to the fireplace or window; or in a kitchen, dark wood set into a poured-resin floor could be echoed by a countertop or cabinets of the same wood. One of the joys of introducing contrasting runners is that it allows you to use luxury materials that in large quantities would blow the budget. Even a sliver of marble, metal, mother-of-pearl, leather, or specialist plaster will add glamour. The only provisos are that the materials are fit for purpose and installed by a professional; the laying and joining must be done precisely and on the correct base, as anything less than a perfect finish will spoil the effect.

OPPOSITE ABOVE

A runner of black carpet webbing makes an unexpected graphic statement in the center of a sheer shade. The same webbing is used to edge a zebra rug for a sense of continuity.

OPPOSITE BELOW

A series of linen panels has been hung to create an intimate backdrop for a dining area. These are echoed by the two long gold runners that are draped across the table at each place setting. The wenge table and chairs accentuate the strong vertical lines in the space.

LEFT

A dramatic feature has been made of the enormous structural support column that runs from floor to ceiling in front of the staircase in my London home. The shiny black specialist plaster finish, by Polidori Barbera, transforms it into a stunning vertical runner that accentuates the height of the room and plays against the matte texture and warm tones of the subtly highlighted parquet floor.

OPPOSITE ABOVE LEFT

The horizontal grain of a pale wood door is strikingly contrasted with a chic, slim, vertical runner of polished nickel, which is echoed by the long nickel door plate.

OPPOSITE ABOVE RIGHT

A wall of timber veneer slats emphasizes the vertical grid while separating the living area from the marble and bespoke joinery entrance hall behind. The JNL Samara lacquered coffee table also has a cross-shaped stainless-steel runner.

OPPOSITE BELOW LEFT

This bathroom in one of my previous London homes features a stunning floor of taupe-colored milk glass, which has a lovely reflective sheen. The same material has been used for the bathtub surround. A runner of black oak connects the tub to the sink opposite (not shown) and gives the room structure.

OPPOSITE BELOW RIGHT

Taupe marble set into the dark wood floor provides an anchor of contrasting material for the dining furniture. Instead of continuing the marble up the wall, the dark wood is repeated in the form of a backlit floating panel. The circular pendant light echoes the shape of the table and chairs, their curves balancing out the lines and angles of the joinery and frames.

THIS PAGE

Almost a work of art, this simple vertical runner of taupe specialist plaster is enhanced by the placement of three extra-tall glass vases and a central up-down wall light that highlights its textural finish.

GRID, FLOW, ZONE

OPPOSITE ABOVE LEFT

A horizontal band in a darker tone of the wall color has been painted at just about chair-rail height. The effect is continued by the contrasting band of the same taupe-colored linen sewn into the earth-brown linen drapes.

OPPOSITE ABOVE RIGHT

In this bathroom, rustic whitewashed plaster walls have been given an edge by the simple addition of a horizontal runner of contrasting taupe. The collection of vintage books and the clay orchid pot are the perfect textural and tonal accessories, alongside all-important bath oils.

OPPOSITE BELOW LEFT

In one of my early dining rooms, banners of white calico have been sewn onto sand-colored fabric and stapled onto wooden battens to cover the walls. The baseboards, painted white, ground the sand-colored floor. The three panels that make up the simple tabletop have been painted to echo the walls. It is a simple design but very effective.

OPPOSITE BELOW RIGHT

A vertical runner of taupe-colored glass makes a striking feature of a cantilevered toilet.

LEFT

The horizontal and vertical lines of this bathroom are at play here, with a marvelous juxtaposition of colors, textures, and finishes: a slim, brushed stainless-steel runner above the sink slices through a vertical banner of specialist plaster, with its inset mirrored niche.

LEFT

Like a contemporary art sculpture, this bespoke bronze pendant light, which took six months to produce, hangs above my dining table, extending almost to the full 19½ feet (6m) of its length. The three beam-like components are suspended at different heights and staggered. It is a fundamental part of the grid and a key focal point in the space, slicing horizontally through the mid-height portion of the room.

OPPOSITE ABOVE LEFT

Steps leading up to a monastically simple bathroom are separated from the adjoining bedroom by Japanese-style screen doors. The panels set into the dark wood framework are sheer natural linen encased in glass.

OPPOSITE ABOVE RIGHT

In this glamorous bathroom, the curved shapes of the freestanding tub, elegant floor-mounted faucet, and perforated gold Tom Dixon pendant light, hung low, offset the straight lines of the black slatted vertical runner, black-lacquered counter, and beautifully grained taupe marble wall.

BELOW AND OPPOSITE BELOW

In this formal lobby the grid has been used in a dynamic way, with polished marble runners set into black timber flooring to create a network of pathways to help the visitor navigate the space. It also provides a framework against which the reception desk and seating areas (not shown) are aligned. The lighting—a mixture of recessed downlights, floor washers, pendant lights, wall lights, and concealed lighting within the grooves of the slatted timber walls—creates drama and brings out the different textures of the surfaces and materials.

FRAMING

Doors have an important function, separating you from the world outside when closed, or welcoming you into a new experience when opened. Their design deserves special consideration, as it can have a dramatic impact on the mood of a room. Not only do doors offer obvious opportunities to emphasize the grid with their strong vertical and horizontal lines, but they also allow you to alter the proportions of rooms, improve the sense of flow, frame views into an adjacent space, and introduce another decorative surface texture to the scheme.

Doors can be designed to be discreet and seamless but I usually choose to make a feature of them, altering the scale wherever possible so that they are double the width of a standard door and extend from floor to ceiling. Large, imposing doors add drama and instantly make a space feel bigger. Conventionally-opening double doors have a real presence and are a great way to make an entrance, but pivoting or sliding doors are neat, space-saving solutions.

Doors can be paneled, inlaid, studded, louvered, lacquered, mirrored, plastered, or clad with leather, fabric, or paper. Door hardware, too, offers further decorative possibilities. I like to think of these elements—the handles, knockers, house numbers, latches, bolts, and keyholes—as the accessories that finish off a really fabulous outfit.

LEFT

The eye is drawn through this monochrome hallway by a series of bespoke dark wood door frames that emphasize the grid and create rhythm through repetition.

OPPOSITE BELOW LEFT

Similarly, these geometrically carved doors have been aligned to ensure there is a clear vista from room to room.

OPPOSITE BELOW RIGHT

Dramatic black wood double doors open onto a runner, also of black wood, set into a stone floor, leading the way with a sense of theater.

OPPOSITE ABOVE LEFT AND ABOVE RIGHT

Frames can also be created by other means, for a similar sense of definition and drama. Here, this Metropolis fire sculpture by BD Design sits like a black frame on dark oak floorboards (left), while in a bedroom, the sleeping space is separated from the dressing area by a bespoke wooden frame that incorporates a headboard on the far side (right).

GRID, FLOW, ZONE

OPPOSITE ABOVE LEFT AND BELOW RIGHT

In one of my previous homes, a typically narrow London townhouse, I had double-width, floor-to-ceiling sliding doors made in blackened oak to separate the kitchen from the hall, increasing the sense of space and creating a grand entrance. The bespoke door handles are slim panels of nickel, which reinforce the vertical lines of the grid, while the shutters in the kitchen, from my own collection, and the floating shelf beneath the antique mirror in the hall (one of a pair) reinforce the horizontals.

OPPOSITE ABOVE RIGHT

Repetition can elevate the humblest of objects into art. Here, a simple display of identical white ceramic bowls are beautifully framed within the grid of this black wood shelving system.

OPPOSITE BELOW LEFT

Often, less is more: unobtrusive rectangular blackened oak handles blend seamlessly with these simple shoji doors.

LEFT

The wonderful contrasting paneling on this jib door continues on the walls on both sides, so the door almost disappears when closed. When open, the inner dark wood frame creates a tantalizing view of the bedroom beyond, with a taupe plaster wall behind the bed and a dramatic OCHRE horn pendant light.

OVERLEAF

Shoji, made of black-lacquered linden wood in the traditional way, without nails or screws, by Miya Shoji, are the perfect choice to frame the views into this internal Japanese-style garden.

TRADEMARKS

SQUARED

Creating designs that incorporate squares and rectangles is another way to emphasize the grid on a small scale and at the same time bring interest and definition to a room. This can be done in many ways and in various materials, from contrasting panels on a door, to an arrangement of pictures on a wall, to the "windowpanes" in a shoji screen, to the pigeonholes of a display cabinet or storage unit. These elements can all be used to create symmetry and balance within a space.

GRID, FLOW, ZONE

BELOW FAR LEFT

This is one of a pair of vertical runners that flank a bed, drawing all the focus to the key piece of furniture in the bedroom. The stunning design wraps over the built-in bedside table, which is inset with narrow strips of brass, echoed by the Atollo bedside lamps designed by Vico Magistretti. The runner continues up the wall and onto the ceiling, with backlit strips replacing the brass. Note the change in direction of the defined linear grain patterns of the taupe veneer, which contributes to the overall textural picture.

BELOW LEFT

I replaced the conventional doors in this hallway in a newly built apartment with these sliding screens made from leather panels set into a frame of dark wood. The doors add interest, symmetry, and texture to the space, creating the perfect backdrop for the lightboxes by Hans Op De Beeck: *Determination (13)* (left) and *Determination (2)* (right). The same materials are also used in the rooms that lead off the hall, thereby creating a sense of continuity and flow.

BELOW RIGHT

The objects you have on show are only part of the story. The furniture or shelving you choose to display them on, as well as how you light them, are equally important. Here, a simple square grid has been created for one wall of a dining room, with downlit open niches alternating, checkerboard style, with black-lacquered cabinet doors.

OPPOSITE ABOVE

A wall in a guest bathroom has been transformed into a grid of illuminated niches, where a balanced arrangement of metallic and other objects is displayed. The deep white shelves protrude beyond the profile of the wall for additional interest.

OPPOSITE BELOW LEFT AND BELOW RIGHT

Stunning bespoke wall finishes, cleverly lit to bring out the nuances of texture and tone, create quiet glamour and drama in a London dining room. On the left is a broad wall runner made of specialist lacquered veneer panels with vertical and horizontal trim detail in polished nickel, by Kinon. It is lit from beneath with uplights recessed into the black oak floorboards to highlight the surface and create a play of reflections. The surrounding joinery is high-gloss lacquered taupe eucalyptus. On the right is another wall in the same room, where a runner of specialist plaster in a herringbone finish, by Polidori Barbera, continues up the wall from a black oak floor runner set into polished taupe marble. The joinery on either side is the same, with polished nickel handles and clear glass shelves on which to create "floating" displays.

RIGHT

In my television room at home, three shelves, with a horizontal storage unit below, house a collection of books, pictures, and other objects. I designed the moveable unit that connects them, made of narrow runners and frames of the same taupe wood, to slide along, allowing me to play around and square off different parts of the display at whim.

UP & DOWN

Step into another world

TRADEMARKS

A staircase is a great place to make a statement. At its finest, it can be a dramatic architectural sculpture, flowing from floor to floor and lifting a home to a whole new level, but even a relatively modest and simple staircase can be made to look arresting. I consider staircases to be the core and spine of a home, a pivotal part of the architecture that centers the whole and balances its proportions; they are never just about getting upstairs or down. I love to create new staircases wherever possible, as they present an unparalleled opportunity to completely transform the way a space feels and works. I especially love it when they can be the star piece of a design: bold, modern, organic, and sophisticated, with integrated lighting to emphasize their form, and my signature elegant, bordered silk runners to soften their treads.

PREVIOUS PAGE
Whether you are going up or going down, a staircase takes you to another level and to somewhere new, so it is important that its design should both reflect and generate a sense of anticipation and excitement. Here, an elegant curved staircase of molded dark-stained timber and glass panels seems to flow through this London townhouse. The lighter wood treads and risers are covered with a runner of taupe wool carpet, edged with a darker shade of taupe for definition.

RIGHT
In this high-glamour, art-deco-style stairwell I designed for an apartment in China, a dramatic 13-foot (4m) crystal chandelier by Robert Clift streams from ceiling to floor through the center like a waterfall. The glossy surfaces of the white-veined black marble treads and risers, and the intricate herringbone-patterned walls in a mixture of lacquered wood, specialist plaster, mirror, and inlaid brass trim all contribute to the magical effect of shadows and sparkle. A timber handrail tops brass-framed clear glass panels, keeping the effect light and bright.

TRADEMARKS

SCULPTURAL

A staircase is the backbone of a home, supporting it structurally, balancing its proportions, and setting the tone stylistically. Whether your preference is for a light, elegant, sweeping design, a bold, contemporary, masculine feel, a curving organic form, or a gravity-defying feat of floating steps and airiness, the staircase is a central architectural feature that can become a star piece in its own right—sculptural, dramatic, and aesthetic.

Staircases are structurally complicated affairs and top-quality engineering and workmanship are essential, so there is no getting away from the fact that bespoke designs are expensive. But although they come at a price, the impact that can be created by rebuilding a staircase is second to none. In listed properties you are restricted as to what you can change, as you are obliged to retain any historic features. In those cases, decorative touches such as staining the handrail and adding a matching hardwood edging along the wall can enhance, increase impact, and ensure the stairs look sleek and in keeping with the rest of your home.

There are many effective alterations you can make to existing designs that will dramatically transform the appearance and mood of the space. Replacing the banisters and balusters or boxing them in is a relatively simple way to update and improve the aesthetics of a humdrum staircase, as is painting, cladding, or carpeting the treads and risers. One of my favorite treatments for creating a luxurious and glamorous effect is to cover the stairs with a runner of silk carpet edged with a contrasting material such as leather.

BELOW

An overhead view down the stairwell of a grand staircase, custom-built from oak and wrought iron, that winds through the central core of a London house, with specially commissioned bespoke glass and metal lanterns by Kevin Reilly suspended at different levels.

OPPOSITE

The lustrous, organic form of this statement staircase that I designed for a London townhouse looks stunning from every angle. It reminds me of whipped cream, but in finely grained dark wood that has a rich, satiny finish. With a taupe silk carpet runner and discreet lighting incorporated into the recessed handrail, it's the ultimate in contemporary glamour.

ABOVE LEFT AND BELOW LEFT

The textures and curves of this spectacular sculptural staircase, made of ebonized wood with clear glass panels set into the sides, are highlighted and echoed by the spiraling form of the bespoke crystal chandelier by Spina, which hangs through two stories and appears as if it is pouring through its central core.

BELOW AND OPPOSITE

This sleek, contemporary staircase curves its way sensuously through the heart of a chic two-story apartment in a converted hospital building in London. Made of bespoke joinery and softly gleaming black metal, the design was conceived in order to connect all the different spaces together by the ribbons of metal that snake up both sides of the staircase to the mezzanine and along the corridors, thereby linking all the common areas of the property. This was one of the first design decisions I made here, as the stunning structure sets the tone for what is to come. The beautifully grained taupe wood that clads the treads and risers, and makes up the square-panel doors on the second-floor landing, tones with the textured specialist plaster finish on the walls. Discreet spotlights highlight the textures and finishes, while the antique crystal chandelier casts decorative shadows and draws the eye upward.

TRADEMARKS

UP & DOWN

OPPOSITE ABOVE LEFT, ABOVE CENTER, AND BELOW CENTER

Three views of this stunning architectural stairwell in a townhouse show off its crisp lines, accentuated by the shadow-gap lighting, taupe silk carpet runner edged in toning leather, and white waxed plaster finish that contrasts dramatically with the black oak joinery. The sharp lines are complemented by the console table and offset by the curves of the spectacular Swarovski crystal light and the ottoman.

OPPOSITE BELOW LEFT

A similar design in one of my former London homes shows how the recessed LED strip lights producing the shadow-gap lighting make the stairs appear to float away from the wall and highlight the reflective quality of the white waxed plaster wall. I capped all the corners with nickel and added a nickel kick plate to the first riser. The textural mix is completed by a taupe silk carpet runner that softens the blackened oak steps.

OPPOSITE ABOVE RIGHT

These black-stained oak steps seem to float down to the basement of the same house because of the glass side panel, which keeps the effect light and airy. The antique stone pots are a foil to the hard lines of this cool, contemporary design.

OPPOSITE BELOW RIGHT

This elegant curl of a spiral staircase was custom-built in cement and painted white, its design inspired by a plaster shell.

THIS PAGE ABOVE LEFT

With its flowing form, this bespoke staircase, of black-stained oak with glass panels set into the sides, is a sculptural feature of this modern apartment.

THIS PAGE BELOW LEFT

Black iron and glass chandeliers by Mark Brazier-Jones are suspended at different heights through the center of this classic black-and-white stairwell. They increase in size from top to bottom, so they seem to pour through its core, casting dappled shadows onto the taupe walls and ceiling.

THIS PAGE ABOVE RIGHT AND BELOW RIGHT

Two views of the open-tread staircase in my London home clearly illustrate the interplay of vertical and horizontal lines that permeates my designs. These are accentuated by the lighting that brings out the textures and tones of the woods and the dramatic black plaster wall.

TRADEMARKS

THIS PAGE AND OPPOSITE

A seamless blend of traditional and contemporary, the design of this staircase is a lesson in quiet, tone-on-tone elegance, achieved through a perfect mix of textures. We designed the French-style staircase and had it made in wrought iron, with a taupe wood handrail and steps to match the herringbone floorboards. The effect is softened by the circles incorporated into the design of the metal balusters, the luxe silk carpet, and the "waterfall" of crystal teardrop lights by OCHRE, cascading down the wall to the entrance hall below.

MADE TO ORDER

Crafting homes to purpose-built perfection

TRADEMARKS

You should be able to wear your home with the ease of a couture gown. Bespoke design enables you to create such a space, one that is literally cut to fit in all the right places, or even improves on what you've been given. It is that heavenly prospect of creating something that's entirely yours; a design that responds to, and even anticipates, your every need. Whether it is bespoke cabinetry, custom light fixtures, or purpose-made furniture or rugs, the point is, crafting things exactly the way you want them means they will fit and complement your space perfectly. It's also incredibly exciting to be able to specify every detail of a design, from the materials and fabrics used to the commissioning of special details and individual touches. This is the only way to create a truly individual home.

PREVIOUS PAGE

These imposing bespoke shutters by Kelly Hoppen Interiors are a key feature of my glamorous black-and-white entrance hall, drawing elegant vertical lines that emphasize the height of the room. They are made from panels of white-lacquered wood fixed to the floor and ceiling with slim black metal rods that allow them to pivot 360 degrees. So dynamic, so big and yet so simple, they are one of my favorite designs.

RIGHT

Beautiful made-to-order paneled cabinetry, with inlaid sections of taupe leather stitched in a diamond formation and trimmed with strips of brass, houses storage for all the family in a multipurpose games room. The quality of the workmanship and finish is second to none, with the direction of the grain in each panel contributing to the overall textural composition.

MADE TO ORDER

JOINERY

Commissioning made-to-measure fixtures, features, and furniture for your home is one of the most pleasing things about designing from scratch. With careful planning and the right craftsman, you will get exactly what you require, in materials and finishes specifically chosen to work with the decorative scheme of the room.

Custom-made elements—cabinetry, closets, and other storage units; architectural features such as doors, doorframes, baseboards, and chair rails; or floor and wall treatments—will give a space a similar edge as a tailored suit or a couture gown when compared to an off-the-peg version. They allow you to play with texture and focus on detail, incorporating runners, inlaid panels, or trims, and juxtaposing colors or surfaces, as well as adding touches of luxurious finishes such as mother-of-pearl, gold leaf, or leather.

There is something inherently pleasing about a bespoke storage unit, designed to your specifications and tailor-made to meet your requirements. It could combine open and closed storage, for the display of books or collections and the concealment of media equipment and unsightly items, and it can be used to improve the proportions of a room and impose symmetry on it.

With an endless choice of colors, grain patterns, and textures that bring different characters to a room, wood is the go-to material for many. But there are numerous others that deserve consideration for made-to-order items, which can be used instead of, or in combination with, wood: lacquer, veneer, glass, mirror, vellum, linen, leather, mother-of-pearl, brass, or chrome, for instance. Doors or drawer fronts may be concealed or made a feature of; their surfaces can be reflective, matte, opaque, slatted, or paneled, offering the opportunity to juxtapose textures. Carefully chosen handles—whether recessed, oversized, elongated, or discreet—will finish the look like earrings enhance a face.

OPPOSITE ABOVE LEFT

Designs don't need to be ornate to have an impact, as the simple lines of this custom-made dressing area prove. The taupe wood closets, with elegantly elongated integral handles, line both sides of a corridor that leads to a bedroom decorated in similar tones, with the same herringbone taupe wood floor underlining the sense of connection.

OPPOSITE ABOVE RIGHT AND BELOW

Different tones of gray and taupe marble and wood combine in the design of this entrance hall. The intricate closet doors that run down the length of the corridor have been custom-made from taupe wood with a defined horizontal grain pattern. The cut-glass wall lights opposite highlight the relief texture of the Chinese-style, geometric lattice pattern.

OPPOSITE BELOW LEFT

This stunning detail of a paneled wall in a family room shows the exquisite workmanship involved in creating this intricate design of taupe wood with polished brass inlays and trim. The matte black and satin brass wall light is by Stéphane Parmentier.

OPPOSITE BELOW RIGHT

I decided to make a feature of this pair of black steel safes, which were integrated into the design of a wall of storage closets. I love the contrast of their glossy black steel surfaces, which reflect the light, against the seamless finish of the taupe wood doors.

TRADEMARKS

RIGHT

This is one of a pair of custom-made taupe timber slatted doors screening shelved alcoves on either side of a marble-clad wall, with an inset television, in a living room. This stunning design allows intriguing glimpses of the accessories within, lit from above by concealed strip lights.

OPPOSITE

An alcove has been transformed into a glamorous dressing area with the addition of a deep wooden ledge inlaid with a series of slim brass runners repeated elsewhere in the bedroom. On either side of the mirror, with its stunning reflection, Japanese-style slatted wooden panels run up the wall and fold over onto the ceiling. Three pendant lights on either side of the mirror provide flattering side lighting for dressing.

CLOCKWISE FROM RIGHT

Bespoke joinery is a great way to make a design statement. A ceiling-height door has been transformed into a specially commissioned decorative panel of glazed metalwork; a wall of customized shelving creates interest in this double-height living area and draws the eye upward, unifying the first floor and mezzanine levels; the stained-oak panels that make up the double-height doors in this apartment were hand-picked for their texture and markings, which complement the varnished oak flooring, and assembled with alternating vertical and horizontal grain patterns; these fabulous handles were fashioned from patinated bronze, which looks stunning against the oak veneer closet fronts; understated recessed bronze pull handles look chic without stealing the limelight from the beautifully grained stained-oak doors; the vertical grooves and long, slim, recessed handles set into the caramel-colored floor-to-ceiling closet doors emphasize the vertical lines of the grid and add subtle detail to the design.

MADE TO ORDER

OPPOSITE LEFT

Stunning expanses of dramatic dark wood are one of my classic design signatures and I love the instantly chic feel they evoke. This detail shows the linear texture of a vertically grooved bathroom door in a Manhattan apartment. Elsewhere in this home, I used open-slatted Japanese-style shoji screens in the same black wood, but here the slats are enclosed to retain privacy but still create a sense of continuity.

OPPOSITE ABOVE RIGHT

This detail is a brilliant example of how different textures work together to emphasize the grid. The play of horizontal lines is evident on all three of the materials that have been combined to such good effect in the design of a bathroom closet: the dark wood louvered door, the finely ridged surface of the metal door handle, and the slim rectangular taupe tiles on the adjacent wall.

OPPOSITE BELOW RIGHT

A wall of floor-to-ceiling closets in sleek black wood makes a strong design statement that will set the tone for the rest of the decor in the room. Juxtaposing them with a warm, luxe material, such as the taupe silk carpet, just seen here, instantly softens the overall effect. These are sliding doors, which are a good space-saving solution, and the handles are simple, large rectangles recessed into the wood.

ABOVE

The Platner chair from Knoll and custom-made desk of black and white lacquer with smoked-glass legs and polished brass inlays are centered in front of the wall panel of polished Calacatta marble. Wall runners of black oak slats wrap onto the ceiling, making the desk feel enclosed, lit by Melogranoblu glass pendants with decorative tassels. The shelves were custom-made in black oak with back panels in white and yellow lacquer.

FLOORS

When it comes to flooring, practicality is a key consideration—in terms of the cost of the raw material and its installation, its subsequent care and maintenance, and the area you are dealing with. Hallways, for example, see a lot of traffic and therefore necessitate hard-wearing materials that are easy to keep clean, whereas bedrooms often benefit from soft, luxurious flooring such as a silk or shag-pile carpet that is warm under bare feet and offers a degree of soundproofing. It often surprises people that I always decide on the flooring after the rest of the design has been conceived. Once you know the overall color scheme and the combination of materials being used for the walls, window treatments, and furniture, you can select flooring that will bring out their best qualities and finish the space to perfection.

THIS PAGE

One of my signature floor treatments is to combine contrasting hard materials with either a runner or an inset panel. Clockwise from above left are: black oak and white resin; taupe-colored stone and patterned marble; polished limestone slabs and black-stained reclaimed floorboards.

THIS PAGE
Wood is a lovely, versatile flooring material that can be stained, bleached, sanded, or painted. Upstairs at home, I created a calm connecting space, which has the feel of an art gallery with black-and-white photography hanging on white walls and a beautiful taupe oak floor that adds warmth.

SHINE
MAGICAL
METALLICS

The key to adding a little glamour to any space

TRADEMARKS

Metallics are an essential component of any decorative palette because they add a delicious accent of glamour. In the same way that a special evening dress can completely transform your appearance from everyday to exceptional, so, too, can a touch of bronze, gold, silver, or crystal confer a sort of magical fairy dust on a room. Metallics also look fabulous when set against matte finishes or contrasting textures. Consider bronze lamps with shades in iridescent silks and satins that are as magnificent when off as when on; or the polish of gleaming stainless steel set against ebony timber, a combination that accentuates the beauty of both. Metallics can be unexpected, too. Specialist plaster finishes using metallics combine my love for texture, luxe, and shine in one. And antique gold leaf has an incredible luminescence all of its own.

PREVIOUS PAGE

With the egg-like chest of drawers from David Gill below the artwork by Erro claiming center stage, this hallway takes on a gallery-like feel. The chest, designed by Garouste & Bonetti and made of oak silver-plated in bronze, glows appealingly under the soft lighting and complements the monochrome decor.

OPPOSITE

The walls of this master bathroom are clad in shiny Calacatta Oro marble, which has wonderful taupe-colored veining—a color repeated in the oak shelf, custom stained to match. Suspended over it are three Lee Broom cut-crystal and brass pendants. The effect of these decorative accents is doubled by the panel of mirror. It is the unexpected but simple juxtaposition of the ornate lights against the raw marble that accentuates the qualities of both.

GOLD

Unequivocally lavish, gold, brass, and bronze bring a sense of splendor and opulence to an interior. As a wall finish, these are deluxe choices that make a statement, while subtler, more restrained touches add a dash of glamour but don't command all the attention. Warm shades of gold look amazing juxtaposed with dark or honey-toned wood and stone, and especially complement the sand-based family of neutrals—cream, caramel, coffee, and chocolate. As a light-catching accent, gold also looks striking contrasted with jewel tones of emerald, ruby, sapphire, amethyst, and topaz.

THIS PAGE

The textures and tones of this specialist plaster wall finish in metallic gold are brought to the fore by the row of LED uplighters set into the toffee-colored wood floor (left). Enhanced by the lighting, the gold mosaic steps of this indoor pool shimmer underwater, in stark contrast to the rough slate-tiled wall (above).

OPPOSITE

Against the textured finish of the bronze plaster wall in my guest bathroom, my gold-leaf Murano glass owl is displayed to perfection on interlocking cubes of brass, mirror, and black anthracite by Kelly Hoppen Interiors (left). The sensuous shape of a sculpture by Paul Vanstone is thrown into relief by the strong lines of the gold de Gournay wallpaper-covered plinth on which it sits and the runner of black plasterwork behind (right).

TRADEMARKS

BELOW

This spectacular gold de Gournay wallpaper was custom-made for a master bedroom and set into a niche, with concealed lighting illuminating its opulent surface. The solidity of the chunky black timber floating shelf contrasts with the delicacy of the cherry-blossom design. Three textured white porcelain vases of white roses add another feminine touch and complete the picture of East-meets-West splendor—the perfect blend of traditional and contemporary, yin and yang.

RIGHT

Sliding doors from the adjoining study open onto this spectacular swimming pool, which sparkles like a jewelry box. The taupe-veined, white marble pool is inlaid with a central "wave" of gold Italian mosaic tiles, which glisten through the water under the ever-changing light streaming through the windows, with their breathtaking views of the Hangzhou skyline. The specialist white plaster finish on the walls has been textured like the ripples of wet sand.

TRADEMARKS

BELOW

The vast antique gilt frame of this painting by George Romney, *Portrait of the Vernon Children*, stands out beautifully against the polished taupe plaster walls in this living room filled with collector's pieces. The ornateness of the frame is a great contrast to the chunky lava-stone ledge that wraps around the walls and makes a feature of the alcoves.

RIGHT

The simplest touches can make effective contributions to a scheme, such as these amber-colored glass vases of delicate sweet peas clustered on a gleaming bronze Christian Liaigre coffee table that reflects the glass.

OPPOSITE

A glass vase of creamy Calla lilies and my faithful gold-leaf Murano glass owl sculpture are reflected in the vintage polished steel and brass coffee table that was the star piece of furniture in the living room of one of my previous London homes (see also pages 254–55).

TRADEMARKS

RIGHT

A glamorous wall treatment such as this gold specialist plaster finish will always make a statement but is totally unexpected in a bathroom, thereby magnifying its impact tenfold. With the addition of a mirrored wall runner, glass light by OCHRE, and floor-standing urn-shaped sink, the small space is transformed into a magical grotto with a dramatic wow factor.

OPPOSITE

The sculptural gold Rock table by Hudson Furniture is a fabulous accent in this elegant living room, gleaming against the warm tones of the earth-colored linen upholstery on the Christian Liaigre armchair and the black wood floor.

SILVER

Cool, modern, and chic, silver accents of chrome, nickel, stainless steel, mirror, and glass add excitement to monochrome interiors and enliven taupe schemes—two of my favorite color palettes. Black-stained timber and materials with gray undertones, such as slate, polished concrete, gray limestone, or marble, instantly look more elegant and animated with the addition of any of these shiny or brushed silvery finishes. Combinations such as a crystal chandelier hanging low over an ebony coffee table, a thin strip of chrome running lengthwise through a taupe-lacquered door, or a polished nickel drawer pull on a gray leather-clad chest, all contribute to the textural layering in a stylish harmonious space.

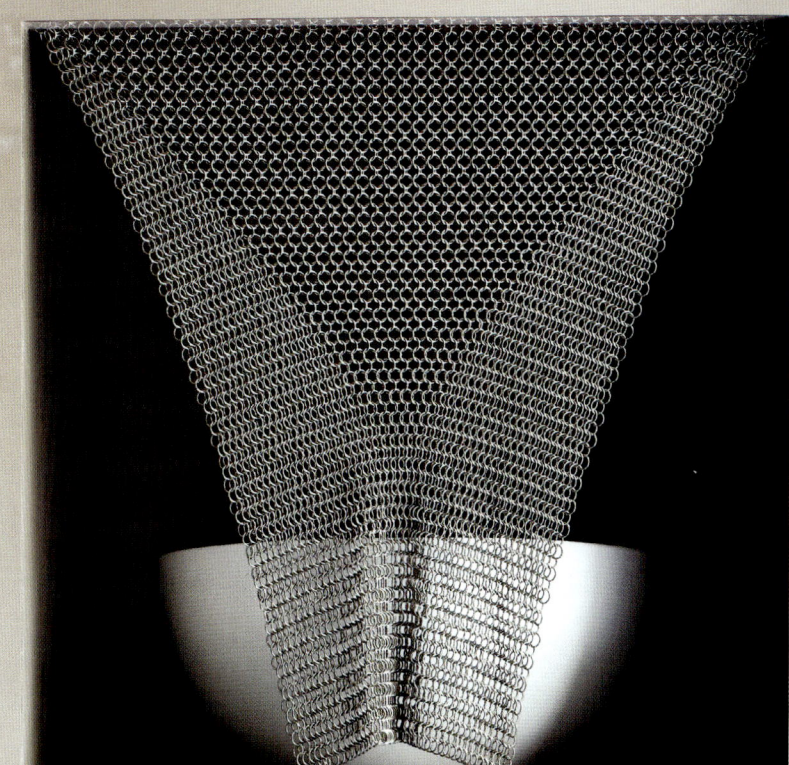
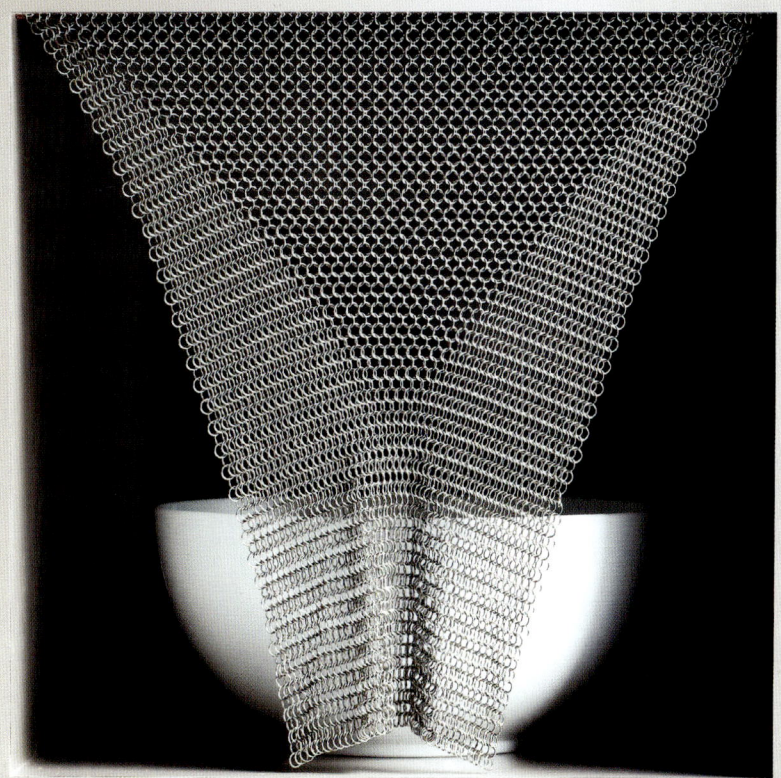

OPPOSITE

The focal point of the kitchen in one of my previous houses was this fire sculpture by BD Design, set into a chrome-framed fireplace high in the wall opposite the kitchen island. Shiny nickel pendant lights provide task lighting for the cooktop (not seen) and complement the fireplace frame.

ABOVE

A shiny white-lacquered timber support column with chrome-edged niches housing a display of mirrored fishbowls makes a strong statement. It is one of several similar columns that help to delineate the different seating areas in a vast open-plan living space (see also pages 262–65).

RIGHT

I designed this open kitchen storage unit for Smallbone. It is made of taupe lacquer with a chainmail curtain hanging over the front of each shelf, adding another interesting texture.

TRADEMARKS

BELOW

This welcoming, elegant living room, decorated in shades of pale gray and taupe with silver accents, really comes alive because of the richly layered textures. It's all about juxtapositions, like the one between this fabulous silver Robert Kuo floor lamp and the black wrought-iron side table by Christian Liaigre, with the soft-weave linen upholstery behind.

RIGHT

The wall behind the Agape porcelain bathtub is clad in pale stone flanked by runners of beautiful silver-ridged tiling (one seen). The dimpled surface of the silver metal table by Asiatides gives another injection of texture, while the chrome towel rail and faucets add more light-reflecting accents.

OPPOSITE RIGHT

These organic-shaped, textured metal wall lights by OCHRE cast light and shadows in all directions, highlighting the brushed-silver frame of this amazing photograph by Ron van Dongen and echoing the shape of the bent flower stem.

SHINE

OPPOSITE LEFT

A folding metal mesh screen from Monpas makes a strong contrast with the dark wood floor, while its rigid structure plays against the soft drape of the open-weave curtains behind.

OPPOSITE RIGHT

The mirror-like surface of the sculpture from Megaron reflects the combed finish of this specialist wall finish made of textured plaster, marble dust, and natural pigments.

LEFT

This gleaming nickel faucet from Dornbracht stands out like a contemporary sculpture in front of the chiseled marble wall.

ABOVE

The mirrored mosaic tiles on the frame of a Bombato mirror by Davide Medri are the perfect foil for the soft-gray textured plaster wall.

TRADEMARKS

BELOW

The mirror-coated surface of the hand-blown Fluid pendant lights by Beau McClellan reflect the interior and help to bounce light around the space. They are all suspended at various heights for a dynamic effect.

RIGHT

I hung a curtain of chainmail at the kitchen window of an apartment in a converted school building where I used to live. According to the principles of feng shui, the hundreds of tiny metal balls that make up the chainmail reflect energy back into the room.

OPPOSITE LEFT

The eye is instantly drawn through the open door of this bathroom by the stunning Molten mirror suspended on the outside of the opaque glass shower cubicle. Designed by Christopher Guy, the silver frame was carved from a single piece of hardwood in an open organic design that looks like molten rivulets of metal.

OPPOSITE RIGHT

Vertical stripes of mosaic tiles in a similar tone but a different texture—metallic silver with a taupe and gray combination—have been used to create a stunning wall covering in a shower room.

PEARL

Mother-of-pearl is one of my most iconic accent materials. Its soft sheen makes it look almost lit from within and I love the understated glamour it brings to a space. Like a string of pearls lighting up a face, mother-of-pearl details make an interior glow with warmth and life. With its various delicate tones of white, cream, gray, blue, pink, and apricot, pearl complements many other materials and works well with numerous color palettes. This versatile accent can be used to add textural contrast in many ways—as an inlaid panel or runner within a wall, tabletop, or other surface, as mosaic tiles, as oversized buttons on pillows, or as accessories such as boxes, picture frames, or vases.

SHINE

OPPOSITE LEFT

Pearl and glass make an unbeatable light-reflective combination, and the honeycomb pattern of these pearlized vases catches the light in interesting ways and adds subtle texture to the space.

OPPOSITE RIGHT

This is a detail of a horizontal band of mother-of-pearl that I had inlaid into an oak wall at the top of a spectacular circular staircase.

LEFT

I love to use mother-of-pearl buttons to embellish pillows, but here they have become objects of desire in their own right, scattered across a shallow petal-shaped bowl. Artfully lit from above, the shiny buttons and silver bowl can only be admired against the dark wenge tabletop.

ABOVE

I have always been known for my precise configuration of pillows and the textural mix that can be introduced by them. Four to six is the perfect number for a bed, and these examples, in shades of taupe in metallic linen, shag-pile, and velvet, graduate from large at the back to small at the front. Oversized mother-of-pearl buttons complement the color palette and add the final layer of texture.

TRANSPARENT
It pays to be reflective

TRADEMARKS

I love to play with transparent materials such as glass, vellum, Plexiglass, crystal, and even acrylic. Transparency is about manipulating light, not through reflection but through the more subtle art of diffusion. It can soften light in a number of ways that add delicate and new experiential layers to a room. Transparent materials are the teases and temptresses of the decorative palette, allowing me to toy and play with ideas of light and shade, shadow and solidity. It is both the sensuous delight of sheer curtains pooling onto a rough stone floor, and the liquid translucency of barely-there furniture. It also enables illusion. Using transparent materials means you can dissolve divisions between rooms with see-through screens, or blur the edges of certain pieces, making them sit more lightly in a room, which is a great trick to employ in smaller spaces.

PREVIOUS PAGE

These incredible acrylic and driftwood blocks by Bleu Nature are great textural pieces to add to an interior, as they combine rough with smooth, solidity with transparency, and ancient with contemporary, all in one piece. Here, set on a beautiful taupe silk carpet layered on a pale wood floor, next to a gray damask sofa, the building blocks of the textural palette are evident.

OPPOSITE

Eero Aarnio's Bubble chair is a mid-century classic and I often include contemporary interpretations of this iconic design as star pieces, to add to the textural mix—in this case linen, white lacquer, and wood—and to introduce organic curves to juxtapose with the straight lines and hard edges of joinery and other furniture. The chrome-edged acrylic forms reflect light and their transparency plays against other solid surfaces.

LEFT

I love the elegant curves and delicate form of this wrought-iron and glass floor lamp—the Sera Lantern, by Mark Brazier-Jones. It moved with me from my previous home and I've chosen to position it against one of the massive wood-clad support columns in my living area, as the dappled shadows it makes are beautiful against the grain pattern of the wood.

ABOVE

This is another perspective on the stunning stairwell lighting seen on page 87, below left, here looking down into the marble-floored entrance hall with its black-lacquered console table. Custom-made by Mark

Brazier-Jones, this is the largest in a series of chandeliers that are hung at different heights through the central well, with the smallest at the top. This view clearly shows the workmanship involved, with each glass disc and ball wired together and onto the black iron framework. The stippled light gently highlights the surrounding surfaces.

RIGHT

Glass chandeliers are sculptural objects in their own right and produce a wonderful play of light and shadow. The organic quality of this Lord Carter chandelier, also by Mark Brazier-Jones, is offset by the edgy slashed linen shade in Stephen Webster's flagship jewelry store.

TRADEMARKS

WEIGHTLESS

The effect of light—both natural and artificial—on the surfaces and textures in an interior has a dramatic impact on the overall mood of the space. Light falling on different textures is absorbed, reflected, or diffused in varying degrees, depending on the quality of the materials in question. This influences how colors are seen and also contributes to the effects of light and shadow, which create drama and atmosphere.

The aim with any interior is to be harmonious and balanced, and one way of achieving this is with a textural mix that adds to the effects of light and dark, transparent and solid. Whether in the form of furniture, shelving, lighting, or accessories, transparent materials such as glass—clear, etched, or sandblasted—Plexiglass, and acrylic all bring a sense of weightlessness and light to a space, as they don't obstruct a view or block the light.

RIGHT

One aspect of the clients' brief for the design of this London townhouse was to create an elegant canvas for their art collection. I had these glass box shelves built into the alcoves in the master bedroom, creating open display cases to house an antique figurine and other treasured pieces.

OPPOSITE LEFT

Clear glass was chosen for practical reasons for the sculptural display cases in jewelry designer Stephen Webster's flagship store. The triangular modules have been put together so as to create an organic curve, with the straight edges and angular forms of the glass playing against the curves of the wood cabinet beneath.

OPPOSITE RIGHT

I designed these glass display cases as a contemporary and unobtrusive way to store a client's collection of antiquarian books. The textured plaster wall makes a perfect neutral backdrop for the books, which seem to float against it.

ABOVE

With light and water playing across its surface, a bespoke screen made of glass bricks by Kelly Hoppen Interiors appears like a mirage—an attractive device for separating a barbecue area from the rest of the outside space.

ABOVE RIGHT

The strands of crystal drops from a Spina light hang like a curtain behind an organic-shaped table by Robert Kuo. The shimmering reflections it makes on the glossy lacquered surface add a magical feel to a bedroom.

BELOW RIGHT

Matte and shiny textures are perfectly balanced in this kitchen combination of Andrew Martin's acrylic chairs with seats upholstered in taupe plastic and a white-painted oak table, both grounded by the dark wood floor.

OPPOSITE ABOVE LEFT AND BELOW LEFT

The apartment I owned in a former school had an open-plan living space with soaring ceilings, so I suspended this Bubble chair by Eero Aarnio to provide a punctuation point between the kitchen and living areas; its transparency means it doesn't block the view (above). A detail of one of the Bubble-style chairs on page 129 highlights the wonderful contrast of the shiny surface with the texture of the linen cushion inside (below).

OPPOSITE ABOVE RIGHT

A solid glass sphere sits, crystal-ball-like, on a black oak newel post, reflecting the chandelier suspended above (see also pages 87 and 130–31).

OPPOSITE BELOW RIGHT

Transparent furniture, such as this glass Ghost chair by Cini Boeri for Fiam, creates an unexpected marrying of solidity and translucency.

TOUCH
inject essential warmth or coolness to any scheme

TRADEMARKS

I always say that designing with fabrics is like cooking with spices. It's the combinations that make them work: consider coarse linens with delicate silks, dense velvets against translucent sheers. Here, the sum is definitely greater than the parts. For example, you could take a beautiful Fortuny silk, but it only really becomes exciting to me if you shock it with a piece of burlap, or even toweling if used in a bathroom. My philosophy is to take what is safe and then add a twist to it. For me, texture and tactility are what really give a space soul. A room must feel good, thrilling your fingertips and teasing your toes, as well as look good, and so fabrics, alongside the hard finishes for each room, are integral to all of my designs from the very beginning. When I start a new project I gather together all the materials, colors, and finishes I want to use before I decide where to use them—assigning them to drapes, furnishings, accessories, or even flooring comes later.

PREVIOUS PAGE

Mixing up textures within a scheme is a true hallmark of my style of design, creating drama in the unexpected pairings and harmony in the yin-yang dynamic as they intensify and balance out each other's qualities. Ripped or slashed fabric, such as this linen scrim shade in Stephen Webster's jewelry store, gives an irreverent twist to a conventional material, here paired with a glossy wood sill and damask upholstery.

OPPOSITE

Without textural contrast, neutral and monochrome interiors look dull and lack the vitality that makes them welcoming places to be. The elegant curves of this chair are enhanced by the ribbed cotton upholstery that extends all the way down its legs, while light filtering through the geometrically cut-out curtain behind throws patterns onto it and the wool carpet.

OVERLEAF LEFT

On a contemporary roof terrace, this wall of water designed by Randle Siddeley takes texture to a new level, especially when juxtaposed with palms.

OVERLEAF RIGHT

A high-shine metal mantelpiece with a cascade of chainmail makes a dramatic and unusual focal point as a faux fireplace.

TEXTURE

The textural mix introduced on surfaces, furniture, furnishings, and objects plays a large part in defining the overall mood of a space. Materials such as coarse linen or wool, distressed wood and stone create a rustic, organic feel very different from a palette of polished plaster, dark wood, lacquer, and leather, which creates a chic, urban vibe. Different textures will inject warmth or coolness into a scheme, too. Consider the effect, both on the eye and to the touch, of a deep-pile silk carpet, a cashmere throw, and velvet pillows, compared to a polished marble floor, a glass tabletop, and silk drapes.

CLOCKWISE FROM ABOVE

The organic twists of the branches are silhouetted against the white wall, while the rough stone pot contrasts with the smooth wood. Marble globes are a foil for the charred bricks and slate hearth of a traditional fireplace. The transparent and reflective qualities of the glass vases are accentuated by the enclosed roses and almost invisible shelf. The unexpected mix of wire, ceramic balls, and silver ceramic side tables bounce off each other, the linen chair, and silk carpet. Purple glass vases gleam smokily against a marble wall, while the lilies echo its white veins. Buttery suede ottomans on shaggy sheepskin on silk carpet are the ultimate in tactile textures.

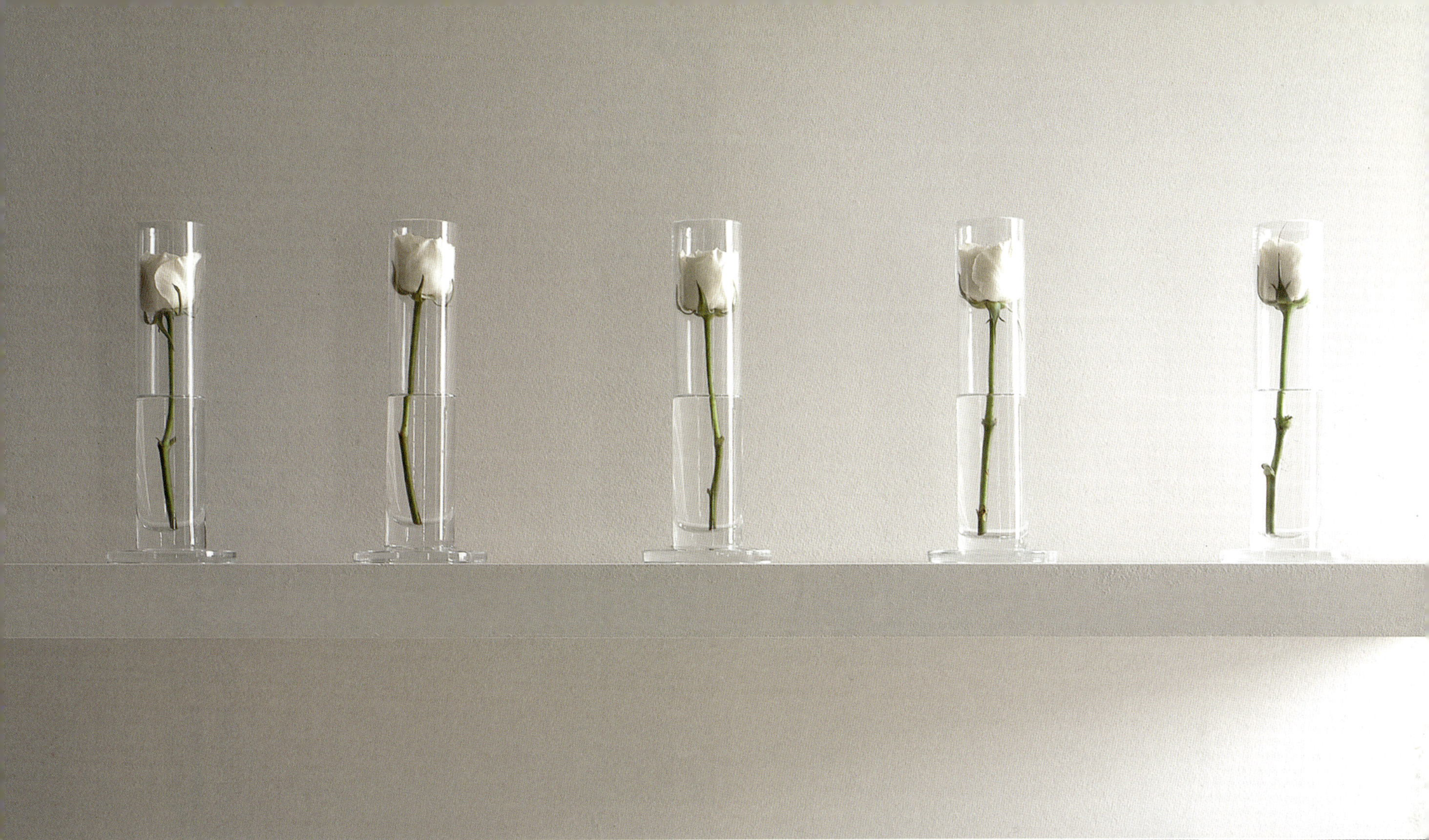

TRADEMARKS

TEXTILES

Creating bold juxtapositions and interesting mixes of materials, finishes, fabrics, and forms is a process that underpins my work at every level. The art of good design is about finding a collection of tones and textures that sit comfortably together and enhance the characteristics of one another. Playing around with samples of paints, surfaces, and fabrics is essential to see which combination produces the harmonious effect and mood you are aiming for.

Building up a fabric story with a pleasing balance of tones and textures is a great way to add layers of comfort and character to a space. It is the first element I consider when I am designing a room, as it is what sets the mood, color palette, and textural interplay that inform the dynamics of the other ingredients. Linen is nearly always the foundation material, as it provides such a good base for any decorating scheme and works well in combination with so many other fabrics, from glamorous silk, lace, and velvet, to luxe leather, suede, and cashmere, to earthy tweed, mohair, and felt. Linen comes in a variety of weights and finishes; it may be soft, rough, coarse, sheer, glazed, metallic, damask, or printed.

Once you have a family of fabrics that you love, you can begin allocating them to different uses, bearing in mind color, texture, drape, and practicality. Decide which are the dominant fabrics—large expanses such as sofas and drapes are generally best kept plain and neutral—and then allocate another for a statement chair and others for trims, borders, pillows, runners, and bands. The textural laws of opposites attracting applies: a silk trim on a wool throw, a velvet band around a damask pillow, or an open-weave curtain over a glazed-linen shade are particularly effective.

RIGHT

Bronze mesh fabric has been layered over a natural linen drape, so its soft tones, which tie in with the wood floor, are visible through the open weave.

OPPOSITE ABOVE LEFT

Adding warmth and comfort, the caramel stripes of this velvet-and-linen cushion match the chair's cane seat and echo the lines of its wood frame.

OPPOSITE BELOW LEFT

A central runner of textured taupe leather brings a luxe quality to the pull-out drawers of a black wood storage unit.

OPPOSITE RIGHT

The fine texture of unlined linen is brought to the fore when light shines through it and doesn't conceal the wooden grid of the French windows.

TRADEMARKS

BELOW AND RIGHT

A rich, dark palette is made luxurious and glamorous by the choice of fabrics. The banquette is upholstered in damask, with cushions and pillows in tactile silk velvet. The close-up of the damask upholstery (right) shows the effectiveness of the cross-stitch detailing, a traditional upholstery technique for marking the position for buttons to be sewn on. Here, it is simply used to add another layer of texture.

OPPOSITE LEFT

A monochrome scheme is enlivened by the use of black lace to overlay cream linen pillows, creating a whole new texture that is both sexy and playful, especially when combined with the self-patterned upholstery.

OPPOSITE RIGHT

The subtle sheen on the black silk seat of this 1930s-style Italian stool complements the glossy finish of its honey-colored wood. Its simple curves echo the intricate latticework of the antique screen behind, which is wittily repeated by the embroidery on the linen pillow.

STAY
Always exciting,
NEUTRAL

TRADEMARKS

I passionately believe that a palette of neutrals—whether taupe-, sand-, or cream-based—can provide a serene and harmonious backdrop against which to layer the color and activity of your life. I like the way they make me feel, as much as the way they look, which is why I have made them my signature colorway for the past forty years. I believe they are the perfect antidote to our frequently oversubscribed schedules and perpetually shrinking amounts of downtime. But whichever family of neutrals I choose to work with on a project, textural contrast is always absolutely key, in order to add richness, depth, and character. It is true that, if used badly, neutrals can be flat and unexciting. But when layered with differing tones and textures, they can be warm or cool, calm or dark, and they are always elegant, refined, sophisticated, and sexy.

PREVIOUS PAGE

The soothing shades of off-white and gray set the tone in this Zen-like living room, where the textures of the materials and the placement of the objects are working in harmony. Balance is created by the shapes and configuration of the three black-and-white photographs of roses, the two linen-covered chairs and the grid of six glass bowls of rose heads and pussy willow stems on the marble tabletop.

OPPOSITE

This master bedroom has a mouthwatering combination of taupe materials at play. Slatted timber panels add texture to the wall and emphasize the grid, while the backlit slatted runners create a backdrop for the wall-mounted bedside floating shelves. The runners wrap over the ceiling, defining the grid overhead. The bed base and headboard are upholstered in rich taupe leather, which offsets the silver-leaf wallpaper and linen bedcover. The white glass and metal mesh pendant and the leaf-lined glass bowls of roses add further color accents and textural layers.

HEROES

Interesting textural combinations are what make neutral schemes sing, as the various qualities of the different surfaces, weaves, and grains absorb or reflect light in different ways and create subtle variations of tone and pattern. One of my favorite ways to juxtapose textures is to use pillows with contrasting bands, which can be placed on everything from leather benches or linen sofas to beds. Bands may be single or layered, wide or narrow, horizontal or vertical, and great fabric choices are velvet, silk, and linen.

CLOCKWISE FROM ABOVE

A taupe linen bench is complemented by a paler taupe pillow in linen with a matching band, topped with a narrow band of white silk velvet. An organic pattern cut into a stone sink for the water to run through creates interest in a neutral bathroom. Delicate patterning and subtle texture are provided by the grain of the whitened floorboards and the white lacy curtain. A similar curtain filters the winter light in a Swiss chalet bedroom. A taupe linen pillow with a wide band of cream velvet adds the finishing touch to a Baltus frame chair upholstered in pale linen. A cream ostrich-leather headboard is offset by simple, crisp bed linen. An off-white linen pillow with a wide taupe velvet band adds tactile luxe to a taupe linen sofa.

TRADEMARKS

BELOW

Carefully composed layers of textures in taupe, cream, and silvery gray work in harmony to make up this comfortable and elegant living room. The seating is upholstered in a sensuous mix of silk, linen, and mohair, with pillows in silk velvet and linen. The shiny surfaces of the Robert Kuo metal floor lamps and the taupe-lacquered coffee tables from kellyhoppen.com play against the matte walls and floor, while the matte bone-china pendant light by Jeremy Cole adds a fabulous spiky focal point.

OPPOSITE

Another view of the same room shows how the subtle patterning of the herringbone oak floor, white mesh sheer curtains, and custom-made table by Robert Kuo, which appears to be made from a stack of concentric discs, plays against the taupe silk drapes, matte walls, and mohair-upholstered Holly Hunt Darder Wingback chairs.

COOL

I have always loved the chic elegance of a monochrome interior, which takes on the stylish quality of a black-and-white photograph in which every element is perfectly framed and balanced. Encompassing the entire scope of black and white tones, and everything in between, it is a palette that goes with everything, in which neither one extreme dominates the other. The result is an easy yin-yang equilibrium as the different tones contrast with, and set each other off, to great effect. Introducing layers of texture is essential to enhance the subtle interplay of light and dark that creates a sense of drama and enlivens the space.

ABOVE

Creating a sense of flow from one room to another results in a coherent atmosphere where nothing jars or is out of place. This dining room and adjoining hallway have been decorated in a monochrome palette featuring many of the same materials and elements to ensure a seamless connection, with the dark wenge dining table echoed by the tall wenge side tables and black-and-white artworks displayed on white walls.

OPPOSITE

A fabulous combination of woods, linens, and marbles in neutral tones of taupe, off-white, and charcoal is accented with clear glass and grass stems. The walls and floor of this living space are both clad in taupe timber, and the chic side table, alongside the linen sofa, was custom-made by Kelly Hoppen Interiors in a mix of black marble and taupe wood with inlay detail. It perfectly sets off the wonderful Globe table lamp by Lee Broom, which is made from a half-sphere of Carrara marble, topped with a lead crystal dome.

WARM

Shades of cream and sand have yellow undertones and tend to be described as "warm," whereas neutrals such as white, gray, and taupe are harder to classify in this way. Taupe encompasses many shades from mushroom to gray-purple, which all work harmoniously with white, black, and silver, but don't sit comfortably with sands or warm-toned woods. The choice of textures evokes warmth or coolness in an interior and these can be changed seasonally, along with accent colors. Velvet, fur, and cashmere are ideal for the winter months, while linens, cottons, and sheers have a lighter feel.

CLOCKWISE FROM ABOVE

Layering pillows on beds is a design signature of mine and here, one in dark taupe velvet supports a smaller one of ivory linen with a silver silk-velvet band. A geometric statement is made by the grid-like padded headboard, the horizontal stripes of the horned buttons on the oblong linen pillows, and the spot design of the knotted quilt. In this chic bedroom, black bamboo flooring, black shutters, and black custom-made joinery and furniture harmonize with pale gray walls, silvery furnishings, and glass accents. Pillows in toning knits and linen with a faux-leather band bring warmth and comfort to this bed, set against a rustic wall.

CALM

Neutrals provide the perfect quiet backdrop for any room, offering a blank canvas in spaces where you want to bring in bold color accents, furnishings, artworks, or star pieces; but, where there is also a carefully curated textural mix, they contribute enough interest in their own right. Calming and harmonious, bedrooms decorated predominantly in neutral tones can be luxurious, sensuous, and eminently relaxing.

CLOCKWISE FROM LEFT

The stars of this bedroom are the headboard of sueded buffalo, also used as a border on the silk carpet, and the oversized Spina crystal chandeliers hung as bedside lamps. Horizontal and vertical narrow bands of taupe silk on white linen pillows make a simple but dynamic detail. A crystal wall light highlights the surface of the specialist plaster finish within the niche, emphasizing the grid. I love using pairs of pendants as bedside lamps, and these scripted glass examples by Alison Berger for Holly Hunt add another layer of texture. This luxurious bedroom is dressed with a rich mix of linen, velvet, satin, cotton, and silk, with glossy lacquer side tables, crystal pendants, and a specialist plaster runner behind the bed. Taupe and gray linen and glazed raffia fabrics give understated shifts of tone and texture. A pair of satin-and-chenille pillows stacked on a velvet ottoman create a more blatantly contrasting textural story.

THIS PAGE
Everything about this perfectly balanced bedroom reflects the grid, from the contrasting bands on the pillows that flow into the runner on the bedcover, to the lines of the textural plaster niches, to the geometric pattern of the wall finishes in the main living space, seen through the internal window (see also pages 252–53 and 288–89).

DARK

Rich tones of bitter chocolate, charcoal, and black make sharp, chic interiors. It is the quantity in which these dark, dense colors are used that affects the mood of the room, taking it from defined and smart in small touches to moody and cocooning when used in greater expanses. Dark colors will naturally make a room feel smaller, but this can work well in bedrooms, which need to feel cozy and nurturing, as well as in dining rooms and bathrooms. The materials used will also have a dramatic effect, as matte textures absorb the light, whereas shiny ones reflect it.

CLOCKWISE FROM LEFT

Two views of this smart bedroom illustrate how to balance light and dark. The pale bedcover and walls are contrasted with the black wood shutters, joinery, and bedside tables. The headboard, with its dark wood panels on either side, is echoed by the chocolate pillows with their wide white bands. Dramatic contrasts of color and texture arrest the eye, such as a shiny black horn button on a cream linen pillow and mother-of-pearl buttons on sumptuous chocolate velvet. In this bedroom, dark wood joinery is contrasted with the pale velvet bedcover and linen headboard, along with the feature ceramic Aloe Shoot pendant light by Jeremy Cole.

CLOCKWISE FROM LEFT

Interesting detail can be introduced to rooms by contrasting colors, textures, finishes, and shapes. An organic-shaped dark wood and woven-cane vintage chaise and a bitter-chocolate velvet pillow with an oversized pearl button make a striking focal point. A combination of dark brown velvet pillows and a faux-crocodile bolster on white linen upholstery underlines the characteristics of each material. A white silk-and-linen carpet with a black faux-crocodile border makes a luxurious layer on a gray stone floor. A slim bolster of faux-crocodile banded with bitter-chocolate velvet accentuates the lines of a white and taupe velvet sofa. The wonderful combinations of textures in this bedroom—the black wood paneling and bedside table, glass pendant lamp from Lasvit, Square Panel textured wallpaper from my collection for Graham & Brown, leather headboard, textured pillows and bedcover, taupe marble runner, which is inset with black marble on the floor, and chrome baseboard—all play against each other and emphasize the grid. Three large polished wooden containers from Africa make a simple foil for the gray concrete floor. Taffeta pillows with a cream linen band and mother-of-pearl buttons contrast with the matte velvet and Novasuede upholstery, while their straight lines are offset by the Kelly Hoppen Ring Screen.

OPPOSITE

The stunning Fortuny pleated silk used to cover this chair cascades onto the dark-stained parquet floor like a shimmering chocolate-colored evening gown. Together with the striking black-and-white photograph of actress Glenn Close by Herb Ritts (1994), it is the focal point of a hallway.

ABOVE LEFT

A rich combination of linens, silk velvet, and damask fabrics in shades of light and dark taupe has been used for the headboard, bedcover, and pillows, creating a sensuous effect.

ABOVE RIGHT

A chair by Kelly Hoppen, upholstered in pale linen and embellished by a floor-length chainmail fringe, makes an interesting and unusual juxtaposition with dark wood flooring and a wood stool by Bleu Nature.

RIGHT

The rich tones and sheen of the Makassar ebony Aspre lounge chair by Christian Liaigre, upholstered in white leather, add subtle color and detail to this room, in which it is the statement piece.

OVERLEAF

By day, this comfortable Zen-like bedroom is bright and airy, with a soothing combination of cream and taupe fabrics and carpet bathed in the soft light filtering through the wall of dark wood shutters behind the bed. At night, with the shutters closed and the festoon shades lowered, the mood changes entirely and the lighting comes into its own, highlighting the qualities of the different textures at play.

MOOD

MAKERS

You might be surprised to see such a large section on color in my book. Although I'm known for my love of taupe and neutral palettes, I'm not afraid of color. In fact, I use it a lot, as color adds chic, wit, warmth, and drama to any scheme. Nevertheless, it still always amazes me how its introduction can completely change a room, sharpening it and giving it an additional bolt of energy. Like a pinch of fragrant saffron enlivening plain rice, the right shade can spice up a neutral scheme and bring out the very best in all the ingredients. Used on the inside of cabinetry, like a bright silk lining inside a sober suit, color can surprise and delight; when employed as, perhaps, luxurious deep-pile velvet upholstery on a star piece of furniture, color can sing and make a statement. From sulphur yellow, burnt orange, and lipstick red to berry tones or the palest rose and the shades of the sea, color has an unrivaled capacity to be subtle and serene or outrageous and bold.

PREVIOUS PAGE

In an old apartment of mine, a yellow wing chair by Squint provides a pop of color in the otherwise monochrome interior, standing out against the black metal staircase and Ring Screen, designed by Kelly Hoppen, which separate the living space from the dining area behind.

OPPOSITE

Color can also be added in more subtle ways than introducing a yellow object, fabric, or paint to a room. In this display cabinet warm LED strips have been used to light niches within the shelving system, transforming them into soft pockets of light that look yellow; the textural ceramics in the adjacent niches are lit up by 12-volt halogen spotlights.

CLOCKWISE FROM RIGHT

The classic wing chair by Squint is covered with bold yellow velvet, right down to its wrapped legs. A living room decorated in buttery shades of cream and yellow ocher is a warm and welcoming space. Yellow arum lilies, in vases by Anna Torfs, accent this seating area, tying in with the paintings by Pia Fries. The yellow-gold tones of the mesh curtain work well with the polished stone floor and inset taupe carpet. A pair of yellow velvet headboard panels and pillows, along with the patterned linen La Fibule stool, accent a monochrome bedroom. Cylindrical glass pendant lights glow warmly against dark wood shutters. The painted interior of a Moissonnier cabinet adds unexpected color. Color can come from unusual sources, such as the foxed pages of antiquarian books in a glass cabinet. Custom-made shelves have been lit from underneath with LED strips, bathing them in warm yellow light.

SULPHUR

Yellow is a striking color that can be used in many ways and shades to accent different rooms in the home, from the warm glow of artificial light, to the glint of a gilt picture frame, to the bright pop of yellow lilies.

The color of sunshine, spices, sand, and spring flowers such as primroses and daffodils, yellow brings instant warmth or an uplifting splash of vibrancy to interiors. The clearer, fresher shades work well in modern, clean-lined spaces, while the dirtier, burnt tones of mustard, yellow ocher, and gleaming amber glassware suit the retro mood of mid-century style. Warm creams and buttery tones are welcoming and easy to live with, while dashes of gilt and soft gold tones complement classic interiors and antique pieces.

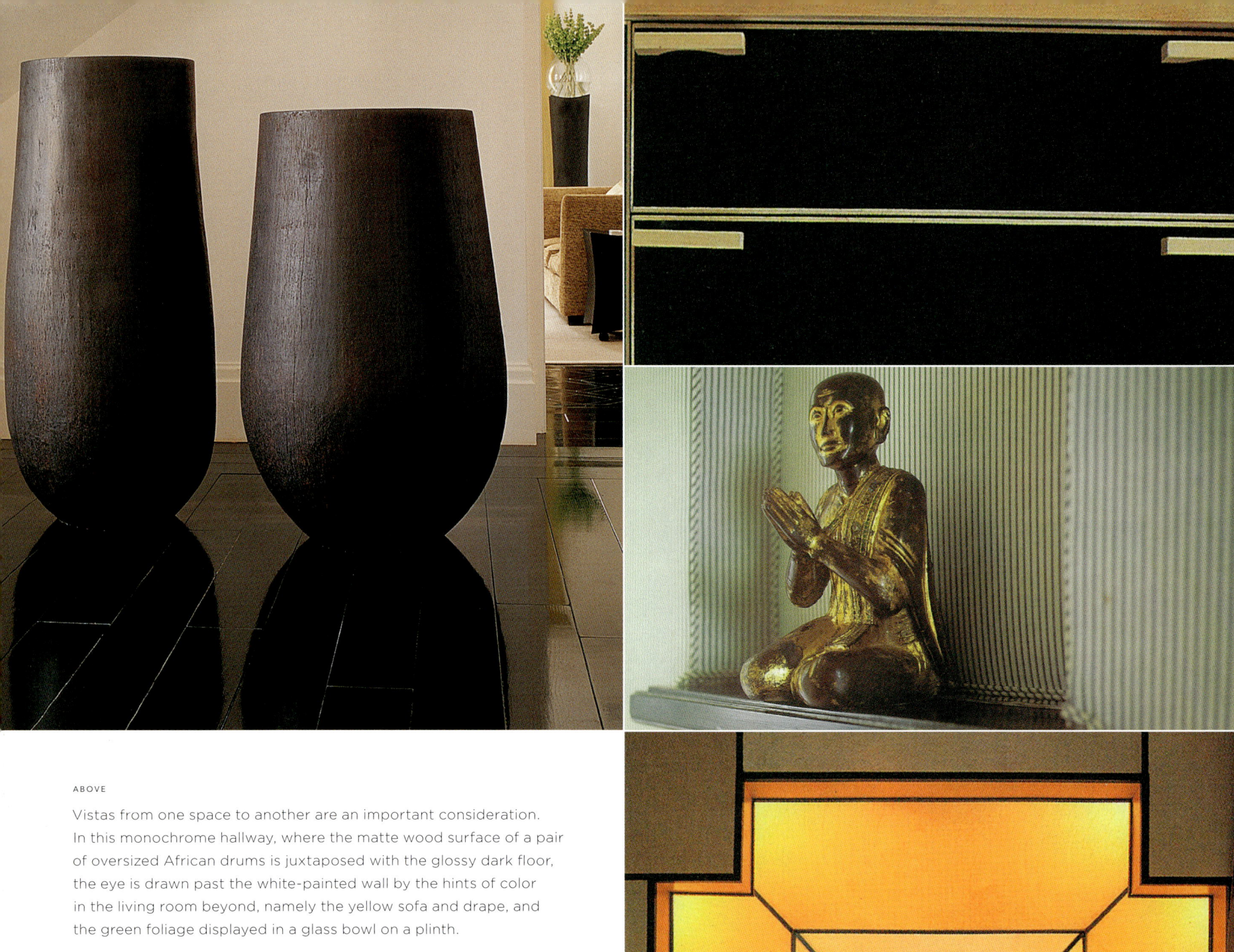

ABOVE

Vistas from one space to another are an important consideration. In this monochrome hallway, where the matte wood surface of a pair of oversized African drums is juxtaposed with the glossy dark floor, the eye is drawn past the white-painted wall by the hints of color in the living room beyond, namely the yellow sofa and drape, and the green foliage displayed in a glass bowl on a plinth.

ABOVE RIGHT

Every detail counts toward the big picture that is formed, such as the fine maple veneer trim on these sleek black-lacquered kitchen drawers, which were designed with classic Japanese style in mind.

CENTER RIGHT

The unusual backdrop to the gold statue of a praying Buddha is utilitarian mattress ticking, which has been used as an inexpensive wall covering.

BELOW RIGHT

In the same Japanese-influenced kitchen shown above, uplighters have been concealed in the ceiling, creating a yellow-toned cruciform feature in each corner, designed by Kelly Hoppen.

OPPOSITE

A detail of the bedroom shown reflected in the mirror on the previous page clearly shows the variety of textures at play—from the white mesh curtain, textured wallpaper, and bedcover to the combination of linen and velvet, dark wood, glass, and white porcelain Bocci lights. The result is a warm, layered room, even with only a simple color accent in the form of the yellow velvet from Abbott and Boyd.

THIS PAGE CLOCKWISE FROM RIGHT

Flowers are a simple but effective way to introduce an accent color, and, of course, they can easily be changed to create a different mood; here, orange rose heads have been scattered in the base of two glass fishbowls and placed on the glossy lacquer surface of a bespoke dining table (see also below left).
The bright orange tones of the lacquered desk in this bedroom (see also left) are echoed in the kilim from The Rug Company and the zinnias in vintage white ceramic vases. Other than the bowls of roses, color is brought into this dramatic dining space—where the stand-out piece is the cascading chandelier of mirrored-glass droplets from Beau McClellan—by the orange-painted alcoves in the custom-made bookcase by Moissonnier.
A palette of white and taupe, with orange accents in the form of a bed runner, pillows, rug, and glassware, is uplifting for a bedroom

CITRUS

Bright and zesty orange makes a great accent for a white room scheme, making the mood light, airy, and fresh, while burnt orange is a pleasing partner for all shades of taupe. Natural wood with gold or taupe undertones is enhanced by orange accents, which can be introduced in the form of glassware or ceramics, soft furnishings or flowers, all of which can be changed easily to alter the mood of a room. Painting a small area, such as a stripe along a wall or a runner along the floor, or the inside of alcoves, niches, or shelves, is a clever and restrained use of color. A painted cabinet interior will also surprise the eye with an unexpected pop of fleeting color when the door is opened.

RIGHT
All-white schemes work well with accents of bold, bright hues, such as this orange silk pillow and the rainbow of colors in the *Moons* artworks by Luca Missoni on the wall behind.

BELOW
At the other end of the same symmetrically designed space, a gridwork of shelving is used to display a collection of vessels and glassware from Bergdorf Goodman; the orange pillows and arum lilies underline the light, uplifting feel of the living room.

CLOCKWISE FROM RIGHT

The dark wood floor of this entrance hall is washed with warm light, while ceiling spots highlight the tan leather of the Christian Liaigre benches. A monochrome room is instantly changed by the addition of an orange cashmere runner and pillow band, and a display of kumquats. A carefully curated combination of wide and narrow stripes in spice tones makes a graphic statement. A display of orange arum lilies in clear glass fishbowls is striking against the wenge console table. An orange velvet pillow with a mother-of-pearl button brings a pop of color to a taupe linen sofa. From above, orange spiral stairs look like an organic sculpture, while lighting enhances the warm tones and grain patterns of the treads. Orange Squint chairs with taupe and black have a harmonious strength, perfect for this mezzanine library. Matte burnt-orange velvet plays against the sheen of black sheepskin.

CLOCKWISE FROM RIGHT
Red suede Gobbi club chairs by Dennis Miller with a row of Flibuste tables by Christian Liaigre form one of two seating zones in an open-plan living area (see also below left). They are positioned on a ribbed silk rug bordered with red embossed leather, in contrast with the dark parquet floor (see also opposite top left). A runner of red Dalsouple rubber set into a white-tiled bathroom floor is continued up the wall behind the tub, in the form of square red tiles, and accessorized with a red stool. Simple displays of red flowers and berries contribute to the texture and color story in a taupe bedroom. The simple lines of a black-lacquered coffee table on a red-striped Kelly Hoppen rug emphasize the grid. Beneath Stuart Redler's artwork, textural red accents are introduced in the form of velvet pillows, glass bowls by Anna Torfs, and flowers. Scarlet velvet and natural linen play beautifully against wood-clad walls.

LIPSTICK

The color of passion, red is an arresting hue that brings energy and vibrancy to a room. It is undeniably glamorous—think of the teasing flash of a Louboutin sole on a stiletto, a crimson lining in a tailored jacket, or a slash of scarlet lipstick. From bright, bold red to deep, rich burgundy, this color makes an eye-catching foil for monochrome palettes. In combination with white it is fresh and bright; set against black, it is bold and dramatic with a distinctive Eastern feel; mixed in with shades of taupe, gray, and cream, it is warm and chic.

ABOVE RIGHT AND BELOW LEFT
A graphic red-and-white, wall-mounted shelf, together with a red leather Massant armchair, bring seductive glamour to a bedroom.

RIGHT
Scarlet padded velvet gives the Meridiani Belmondo armchairs and footstools a plush feel and is the perfect complement to the gray shag-pile carpet and velvet walls of this movie room.

CLOCKWISE FROM LEFT

A scarlet velvet runner and a silk striped pillow add Eastern-style opulence to a bed. A red Sutra Throne chair by Mark Brazier-Jones brings drama and flamboyance to a bedroom. Printed red leather and horsehair cushions add texture and color to a wenge chair. A black-lacquered vase of burgundy dahlias on a Plexiglass table beneath a cylindrical light makes an interesting vignette. Crimson dahlia heads in a Plexiglass tray are simple but dramatic on a black tabletop. Daniel Kelly's artwork, *Topsy Turvy* (2008), brings bold red into this chic dining room, furnished with a Christian Liaigre sideboard and chairs. The linear theme of this seating area is emphasized by the striped rug, red pillows, and tall glass vases of flowers. Burgundy shot-silk bands make taupe linen pillows glamorous.

CLOCKWISE FROM ABOVE LEFT

A dusty-pink chest of drawers with silver detailing adds cool, feminine opulence to a pale gray and off-white bedroom. One of a pair of vintage armchairs, upholstered in pinky taupe silk velvet, sits below a photograph by Louise Bobbe, giving my dressing room a Hollywood-boudoir vibe (see also page 323). White linen drapes layered over white mesh curtains are given substance with a contrasting wide band of matte blush-pink velvet. A stone dish of succulents displays a variety of color tones and is a contemporary way to add texture. Vases of pale pink roses are sometimes the only accents needed, either as a centerpiece on a dining table (right), or on side tables, as in my bedroom (below right). This terrific antique-copper-shelled snail by Robert Kuo is a humorous focal point on a roof terrace. Iridescent mother-of-pearl is one of my favorite textural accents and I often use it in the form of oversized buttons as embellishments on pillows; here, they make a great display in a papier-mâché bowl.

RIGHT AND BELOW RIGHT

Grouping similar items always makes an impactful display: nude-pink roses in a cluster of pearlized containers stand out on a black wood shelf (above); nude-pink textured glassware on a taupe glass shelf brings warmth to a marble and stone bathroom (below).

BLUSH

The soft, calming shade of dusty, pastel pink—the color of vintage silk lingerie—is a color I have started to use more and more and I have become increasingly fond of it. From subtle touches in the form of blush-pink blooms and sculptural succulents to larger and more permanent accents on furniture and soft furnishings, this gentle hue adds warmth and femininity to a scheme based on taupe, gray, or white tones. As with every color, the texture you choose is all-important: shiny glass, metal, or mother-of-pearl add instant glamour; light-reflecting silk velvet, shot silk, or lacquer create a luxe, opulent feel; matte velvet, linen, or paintwork add understated layers of color and texture.

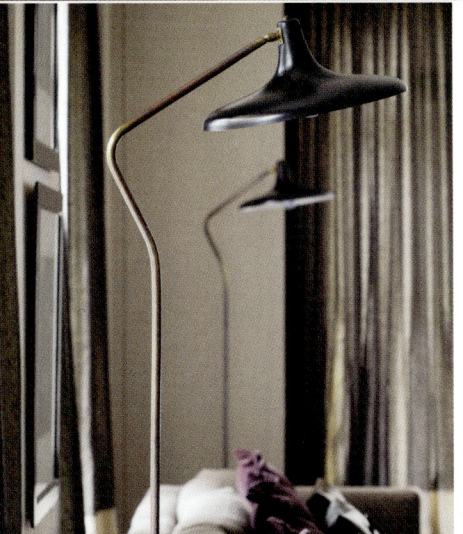

BERRY

Rich and opulent, purple is not for shrinking violets. It's a bold, strong color that instantly brings a luxe feel to a room and is especially effective in sumptuous fabrics such as velvet, leather, satin, and silk. In its purest form, purple and blackberry tones make fantastic partners for dark charcoal, silvery or smoky grays, black, and white, while deep plum and eggplant shades have a subtler effect and are perfect complements for rich mahogany, natural wood, and taupe tones. Mother-of-pearl, bronze, glass, and glossy black finishes are all welcome additions in such color schemes.

CLOCKWISE FROM OPPOSITE TOP LEFT

Purple orchids echo Warren Platner's leather Knoll chair. Purple velvet complements natural linen and gray textured velvet in a bedroom. A violet silk pillow adorns a daybed draped in white voile, a light counterpoint to the studded wenge cabinet from David Gill. Plum glazed-linen upholstery, a velvet band, and a leather rug border are tonally in tune with a taupe carpet and linen pillows. Similar textures and tones are at play on another sofa, but in different proportions. Bronze floor lamps with glossy black shades throw light on a taupe sofa with purple velvet pillows. Plum pillows of silk organza with mother-of-pearl buttons add luster to charcoal upholstery. A purple leather bolster complements a dark gray linen bench. Leather rug borders are a great way to contrast colors and textures.

CLOCKWISE FROM RIGHT

An aquamarine silk pillow band and lampshade bring bold color into a neutral bedroom, with a splash of metallic from the Porta Romana lamp. Gentle seafoam tones with white detailing have been used on the wall paneling in another bedroom. The bedroom shown top right is reflected here in a black-framed mirror. All the objects on the glossy blue table by India Mahdavi in one of my guest bedrooms (see also above left) tie in with the gray, taupe, white, and sea-green theme. This rustic bronze sculpture adds color and emphasizes the grid. Vintage nightstands have been sprayed in sea-green lacquer, and the striped velvet runner picks up all the dark tones in the room. This bedroom palette takes its cue from the artwork by Neil Reddy, with accents of turquoise silk and velvet.

OCEAN

From bright turquoise and aquamarine to shades of almost gray and blue, ocean colors encompass almost as many tones as the sea itself: the clear turquoise of tropical waters under a bright blue sky, the emerald and sapphire depths of a Mediterranean cove, the undulating blue-gray swell of a wintry ocean under low-lying rain clouds, and the lighter, dirtier shade of seafoam on a stormy day. These colors are easy partners for natural materials and neutral tones. They have an innate affinity with water and so work well as accents in bathrooms, pool areas, and home spas, and they are also inherently soothing when introduced into bedrooms.

ABOVE RIGHT AND RIGHT
Organic-shaped ceramic vases from kellyhoppen.com (above right) are a simple way to bring splashes of color into a space, while a specialist wall finish of textured plaster combined with blue-green pigment (right) is an example of a more committed approach to color and texture.

CLOCKWISE FROM LEFT

Shallow nickel bowls of moss and echeveria make a contemporary display. An all-white bedroom is lifted with accents of metal (Tom Dixon's Mirror Ball light), black oak, and green velvet pillow bands and a bed runner. White sheer drapes are trimmed with a deep band of emerald velvet in a monochrome hallway. I decorated one of my guest bedrooms in earthy khaki offset by black and white; this timeless neutral is a fashion favorite and now I'm using it in interiors. Glossy limes look extra vibrant against the marble and brass bowl from Apparatus Studio. The leaves lining this trio of glass containers are showcased against the wenge table with its stainless-steel runner. Moss-green velvet pillows accent a Christian Liaigre sofa in taupe velvet. A green velvet pillow with contrasting linen band complements the white linen cover of the Kelly Hoppen chair, with its long chainmail fringe.

MEADOW

Lush green is perhaps nature's most prolific color in all its tones and shades, from the yellow-green of new spring shoots to the rich emerald of moss, and everything in between. It is an easy color to use with most materials, since it looks as good with all types of wood and stone as with man-made composites, rubber, resin, and Plexiglass. There is a shade of green that will complement every neutral color you can think of. The most obvious and simplest way to bring accents of green into a room is with foliage and plants, which can be used to make striking but easily changeable displays.

CLOCKWISE FROM LEFT

Glass bowls of snake grass are displayed on a line of elegant Modénature wenge tables. A less formal display of hydrangeas in different glass vessels adorns the table in my entrance hall. One of my early designs was this study decorated in lime-green paint and gingham, with yellow and purple accents. Another is this Eastern-inspired dining room in paddy-field green and black on a neutral backdrop, with Carolyn Quartermaine gold-script fabric on the chairs. This display on my landing is a symphony of textures: the beaten metal and marble Christian Liaigre console, the patterned glass vases, and pompom blooms that draw the eye to the husky. Vertical panels of fresh green and white linen are echoed by the pillows and balanced by the horizontal of the silk ottoman. Lush green velvet is juxtaposed with black burlap on a black wood chaise longue.

SHED SOME LIGHT

Good lighting is what brings an interior to life

MOOD MAKERS

Lighting to me is everything. Without it, a room is never finished. Just as the type of music you play at a party will dictate how the party evolves, lighting unequivocally sets the mood and tone of an interior. People can destroy their homes with awful lighting, because without correct illumination even the most well-considered scheme will feel flat and uncomfortable. Conversely, basic furnishings and fixtures can look fabulous if they are lit properly. The trick is to build lighting up in careful layers, and ensure it is adjustable so it can be adapted to every occasion. At its simplest, good lighting combines a basecoat of task lighting, so you can see what you're doing, with mood lighting as the atmospheric topcoat. Star pieces of lighting can be a spectacular addition and are one of my favorite ways to introduce a sense of theater to a space. Sometimes a statement light fixture doesn't even have to be a source of light itself, but can be lit up by concealed directional spotlights recessed into the ceiling, floor, or wall to create drama and atmosphere.

PREVIOUS PAGE

Suspended low over the lacquered surface of a copper-based table by Robert Kuo, this impressive contemporary lantern, Lustre Ovale from Galerie Van der Straeten, is the centerpiece of an entrance hall in a New York apartment. It lights the painting, *I Am Not a Geisha* by Daniel Kelly, while the metal frame casts a dramatic starburst pattern of shadows onto the ceiling.

OPPOSITE

Spectacular lights should look like pieces of sculpture, and still have an impact on a space even when they are not lit. This amazing pendant light is made of tiers of thin white plaster tiles for a contemporary twist on traditional chandeliers of tiered crystal. Like an oversized upside-down wedding cake, it hangs in the center of a circular stairwell.

SPARKLE

Far more than a merely functional element, lighting is one of the most dynamic and versatile design ingredients you can use in an interior, creating pools of light and dramatic shadows, drawing the focus of attention where you want it, highlighting artworks and objects, and enhancing the textures and colors of surfaces and materials. Statement lighting is an amazingly effective way to create drama. Whether antique or contemporary, ornate or sculptural, statement lights can have the impact of artworks even when they are unlit, as well as creating spectacular plays of light and shadow when they are.

Successful lighting design is the result of good planning. Lighting is such an essential ingredient—having a direct impact on mood as well as being a practical necessity—that it needs to be considered at the early stages of any project. A carefully thought-out lighting scheme—drawn up in consultation with a specialist lighting designer for best results—will build in flexibility in order to combine functionality with atmosphere and impact.

ABOVE

Decorative elements and *objets* are a great way to express your personality, and light adds an extra dimension. This lizard-shaped metal and crystal wall light, Lézard Électrique by Mathieu Lustrerie, has pride of place on a shelf, bringing a quirky and humorous twist to a living space.

OPPOSITE

Multifaceted crystal sparkles like nothing else when light shines through it or reflects off its surface. These magnificent spirals of wired Swarovski crystals bring everything I love to a space in a single design—glamour, drama, and impact. I often use these sculptural pieces as the wow factor in hallways or have them swirling through the center of a stairwell.

DESIGN

I always design the lighting for an interior on floor plans and elevations, working out exactly the right balance and where I want each beam or wash of light to fall. Once the surface materials have been chosen and the furniture layout has been planned, I can then decide where I want pools of light in a seating area, where I need to spotlight artworks or provide task lighting over a work surface, whether I want shadow-gap lighting up a staircase or low-level wall lights washing over the treads, whether I want backlighting in a glass-fronted niche or LED strips running along the underside of shelves, and whether I want floor lights, wall lights, or downlights recessed in the ceiling.

Every aspect requires absolute precision. A series of pendant lights suspended over a dining table, for example, need to be spaced accurately to fit the proportions of the particular table, which may, in turn, be placed on an inset panel of contrasting material within the main flooring. The pendants need to hang at exactly the right height to provide flattering, conducive lighting, without blocking the view of people sitting opposite each other.

The most essential ingredient is flexibility, which can be achieved by installing several circuits and dimmer switches for optimum control: a five-amp circuit for task lights and table and floor lamps; a circuit for recess lighting to highlight artworks and walls; a circuit for low-level or shadow-gap lighting; and another for wall lights and chandeliers.

THIS PAGE AND OPPOSITE

Assessing the levels of natural light in an interior is the first step to designing your lighting. The different views shown here of the fabulous, dark lacquer, pivoting-panel doors in my home illustrate how much impact the choice of materials has on light. I designed these innovative floor-to-ceiling doors to divide my television room from my open-plan dining space, and whatever angle they are moved to, their shiny surfaces bounce light around and reflect ever-changing views of the room. Ambient lighting is provided by shadow-gap lighting and directional downlights recessed in the ceiling, while the shelves in the television room and in the kitchen breakfast nook (below left) are lit with LED strips along the underside of each shelf.

OVERLEAF

The cascade of Fluid pendant lights by Beau McClellan seems like an art installation when viewed from the walkway above, with the photograph by Daniel Parker behind. Suspended over the glossy lacquered surface of the bespoke Bellavista table, the hand-blown mirrored glass "teardrops" creates multidimensional reflections that change throughout the day.

CLOCKWISE FROM RIGHT

Jeremy Cole's White Flax pendant light is made up of 350 handcrafted porcelain ceramic leaves, arranged geometrically to distribute the light evenly. It hangs like a softly illuminated hedgehog, bringing a wonderfully spiky texture to a living room.

I used these enormous "floating" bubbles, blown by DARK, to hang in the shades that I designed above the linear coffee tables in my sitting area, where they provide a wonderful ambient light. Being made of clear glass, they don't obstruct views of the room in any direction, and their curves reflect light and balance out the strict straight lines elsewhere in the room.

These glass chandeliers within metal gimbals, by Arteinmotion, have a great presence but still look delicate and light. Suspended at different levels, they are perfect for this double-height space, where they look stunning viewed from above or below.

Melogranoblu's cloud-like formation of hand-blown glass bubbles, lit from above, forms a theatrical light installation over a dining table.

I designed this Kelly Light Sculpture for Spina. Made from crystal, silver chain, and chrome, it hangs from ceiling to floor, making a fantastic decorative feature and an effective zoning device in any room. Here, in one of my old sitting rooms, it lights up a photograph of the actress Jibby Beane by Nadav Kander.

The combination of crystal and light produces a magical effect. These sparkling strands are part of a glamorous light suspended beside a bed. This Lalique-style foor lamp by Mathieu Lustrerie has all the drama and presence of an illuminated sculpture and its beaded texture echoes the mesh curtain hanging behind it.

MOOD MAKERS

SHED SOME LIGHT

CLOCKWISE FROM BELOW

Reflected in a glass table at basement level, this glass and metal lantern is the last of a series commissioned from Kevin Reilly to hang through the center in an oak and wrought-iron staircase. A combination of metal and opaque glass pendants and metal and paper wall lights, both by Kevin Reilly, provide chic illumination in a narrow hallway. Gunmetal steel wall lights by Tristan Auer for Pouenat give soft, diffuse light in a bathroom. The linear bronze light I designed to hang above my dining table emphasizes the grid and balances the bubble lights on the other side of the room. These lightboxes were custom-designed by Kelly Hoppen for the Eastern-inspired hallway, reflecting its white decor and black joinery. Stéphane Davidts's brushed bronze and ivory Chinet lights cast a soft wash of light up and down a hall wall. Tom Dixon's textured nickel-plated aluminum Gem pendants reflect light off their angled surfaces like the facets of a gemstone.

ON REFLECTION

Mirrors bounce light and energy around a room

MOOD MAKERS

Mirrors don't compete in a design, rather they reflect and complete it. They can be the stealth warriors of the decorative design arsenal, capturing light and merging into their backdrops, while quietly transforming, skillfully expanding, and subtly re-energizing their environment. But they can also be magnificent aesthetic statements in their own right. Large mirrors can stand proud on the floor, be framed like precious artworks, or hung in groups. Smaller, wall-mounted mirrors can be cleverly configured in pleasing compositions, in order to gently enliven a room without detracting from the surrounding finishes or being too overwhelming. I think of mirrors as exquisite pieces of jewelry for the home: they are beautiful adornments, whether modern, vintage, or custom-made, adding that all-important finishing touch of elegance and intrigue.

PREVIOUS PAGE

With its mirrored, rippled surface of nickel-plated copper sheeting, the Porta Romana Waterfall wall light frames a distorted reflection of the bed opposite. The pale gray bedcover and pillows on it are uplifted by a pop of color in the form of an aquamarine silk velvet runner, which matches the pillow on the grey Amy Somerville armchair.

OPPOSITE

The graphic lines of the mirror's dark-stained oak frame, at sharp right angles to the black baseboard and parquet floor, are offset by the reflection of the lacquered top and cylindrical copper base of the Robert Kuo table. Set against a silver-leaf feature wall in an entrance hall, the large mirror helps to bounce light around the space and make it feel larger.

MOOD MAKERS

Circles are a symbol of wholeness, completion, eternity, and perfection. Circular mirrors are one of my signature accessories. I use them in groups, in pairs, or singly, depending on the effect I want to achieve. As with all mirrors, they reflect light and energy around a space, and the curved shape is a great counterpoint for the straight lines of the grid. Designs incorporating swirls and scrolls have a similar effect and bring a wonderfully organic feel to a space.

TOP ROW LEFT TO RIGHT

Made up of a series of different-sized circular mirrors with deep metal frames, this design from DK Home is like a reflective art installation, suggestive of dividing cells. Hung opposite ways up on either side of a kitchen doorway, they bring a sense of movement and balance to the space, and soften the lines of the crisply contrasting joinery. The smaller version of the same design, seen through the open door, draws the eye and creates continuity between the two spaces.
This exquisitely carved, gold-finished mirror by Christopher Guy is one of a pair in a hallway, reflecting the open-plan living and dining space opposite, with its Jeremy Cole Aloe Blossom pendant and Promemoria and Kelly Hoppen furniture.
An ornate mirror fashioned from gold-leaf metal circles reflects a pair of gold metallic pendant lights that hang above a dining table, creating an opulent mood for entertaining.

BOTTOM ROW LEFT TO RIGHT

With their distorted reflections of a kitchen, this arrangement of five convex mirrors brings a quirky, dynamic feel to the space. The straight lines of the joinery reflected in this Porta Romana Pioche mirror accentuate its curves and vice versa. Guest bathrooms are great spaces to indulge in a bold pattern, and this bronze sculpted and twisted frame works beautifully on the gold-and-charcoal Botanic wallpaper I designed for Graham & Brown.
An irregular-shaped gold mirror from David Gill, with its extravagant swirls and curves, is an ornate accent piece in a neutral interior.
Deep-framed anthracite metal mirrors in another organic configuration make an ever-changing artwork on the wall of a seating area.

RIGHT

In my entrance hall, a single round mirror, originally found on the side of a railway in Eastern Europe and repainted, softens the lines of the bespoke pivoting wooden shutters that I designed, the black-and-white marble floor, and the sculptural chair by Gallerie 16, while reflecting the walkway through to the breakfast nook beyond.

OPPOSITE ABOVE

Two large convex mirrors flank the doorway to one of my spare bedrooms, bouncing the light around the corridor and creating interesting reflections. The pair of vintage benches below them echoes their curves and reinforces the balanced effect.

OPPOSITE BELOW LEFT

Grouping a series of iron-framed mirrors together on a bedroom wall creates an organic installation, which gives beautiful reflections of the bed and decorative crystal lighting.

OPPOSITE BELOW RIGHT

An oversized floor-standing mirror enhances the feeling of space and light as well as providing a witty reflection of the circular Ball chair.

OBJECTS OF DESIRE

Star pieces to make your soul sing

MOOD MAKERS

The choices you make in a home are integral to the way people react to it; furniture, especially, tells many tales. But art, books, your specially selected artifacts and personal collections are what transform a house into a home. You can create an entire room around a star piece: they are the extroverts of a decorating scheme, the big personalities around which the rest of a design can dance. They can be unexpected and add a touch of drama, or be highly personal, bringing an intimate narrative quality to more private spaces. But there has got to be the right balance of old and new—that's when it becomes exciting to me. I particularly love old buildings with modern things in them. Equally, the right antique or vintage piece can lift a contemporary scheme by injecting it with personality and individuality. What's heaven for me is a Fontana artwork on the wall and underneath it an incredible Bombay chest of drawers or a baroque piece of furniture with an Anglepoise light on it. But sometimes a single empty bowl can look just as stunning in its simplicity.

PREVIOUS PAGE

The objects and art you choose to display in your home are what make it truly personal to you. This artwork by Peter Beard, a photographic piece based on the African landscape, was hung in the corridor opposite the entrance to the living area, making it the focal point that draws the eye as you walk out of the room. The addition of the vast, primitive-looking mango-wood vessel is entirely fitting, while Christian Liaigre's Saline daybed both underlines the artwork with its sleek form and adds balance by introducing a contemporary counterpoint.

OPPOSITE

The fabulous India Mahdavi circular stools, with their faux-crocodile-upholstered seats and organically curved wooden bases, are the perfect pieces to offset the sharp lines and hard edges of the bespoke white-lacquered bar, wrapped with polished chrome bands, designed by Kelly Hoppen Interiors. The great mix of textures and shapes makes this a highly glamorous area, with the haunting photograph of a woman by Désirée Dolron presiding.

CURATED

I am a great believer that every home should reflect the people who live in it. It is only then, with the personal touches that reveal the interests, passions, histories, and travel stories of its inhabitants on show, that a space will truly feel like home. Surrounding yourself with pieces that you love or that mean something to you is one of life's great pleasures, whether they are artworks or precious objects, family heirlooms or collections. As a designer, I love the challenge of getting into my clients' heads, of working out how they live and what drives them and makes them happy. That process is essential for me to design a home that is entirely right for them. There is no greater compliment than when a client tells me they feel as though they have always lived in the home I have created for them.

OPPOSITE
Part of the brief from the owner of this Victorian townhouse was that the design be conceived as an elegant canvas for the display of an art collection. The challenge of marrying the traditional features of the house with the modern art to be displayed in it was met by laying black bamboo flooring throughout, with strong lines created by matching joinery and a simple palette of black, white, and bronze. These shelves were custom-made to display the homeowner's collection of horse figurines.

ABOVE
I love the subtle textures and colors found in a display of vintage books—neutral tones that would work in any interior. Stacked into piles and tied with string, they make an attractive art installation on narrow floating shelves.

ABOVE RIGHT
Chosen well and displayed with thought, everyday objects can be very pleasing to the eye. Here, a collection of brass cocktail-mixing equipment makes a graphic picture on a black-and-white striped marble platter set on a Calacatta marble bar with polished brass inlay detailing.

RIGHT
Four Giacometti-style West African bronze figures from Pebble London are arranged to great effect next to a similar style bronze lamp on a bronze-framed console table, both by Christian Liaigre. Unified by their slender lines and metallic finishes, they are the perfect partners for a successful display.

MOOD MAKERS

DETAIL

Cabinets, shelves, niches, mantelpieces, hearths, or tabletops can all provide settings for interesting displays to add vitality and a sense of theater to your home; the aim is to create a series of still lifes that will stimulate or soothe the eye when viewed from various angles. Strive for balance rather than symmetry—decide on your center of focus and work outward from there, juxtaposing different heights, widths, textures, tones, or materials but using a recurring theme or unifying element to bring everything together.

CLOCKWISE FROM RIGHT

A wooden vessel is beautifully offset by the glass bowl of cosmos: rough and smooth, matte and gloss, hard and soft, solid and transparent, tall and short, fat and slim, in one simple display. A carved wooden artifact on a slim wenge table is the focal point of this dressing room. The ridged metal bowl of moss and succulents is an attractive foil to the mirror and black lacquer coffee table from my collection. Against a marble backdrop, disparate objects are unified by displaying them in identical vessels, while the scrolls of sheet music link with the tall ribbed pot. The dramatic lighting and dark plaster wall finish make this niche the perfect showcase for a pair of textured artifacts. Glass and crystal objects, such as these spheres, make great textural accents and are easy to display in any interior.

OBJECTS OF DESIRE

LOVED

The repetition and arrangement of even the simplest objects can elevate their status to works of art, but eclectic and ornate pieces can also be grouped together to great effect, as long as the display is balanced. Color, texture, form, and proportion should all be taken into account, and then a sense of order can be imposed by arranging a collection in grids, rows, or groups of two, three, four, or more. The Eastern philosophy is to keep compositions fluid and fresh, changing them with the seasons and rotating objects in and out of storage to ensure they don't lose their appeal.

CLOCKWISE FROM RIGHT

Crystal and coral are organic forms that bring a unique energy to a space and I have used them throughout my career for the wonderful texture they bring to monochrome spaces. Here, a quartz section adds sparkle and rough texture to a black oak shelf; the delicate form of farmed coral, juxtaposed with a pair of tall sculptures by Grillo Demo, is in stark contrast to its black surroundings; branching coral stands out against the smooth marble mantelpiece, textured silver wallpaper, and photograph by Louise Dahl-Wolfe. This bespoke glass-fronted cabinet, with its slim, dark wood frame and wonderful textured plaster background, was designed to fit into a shallow alcove in a dining room to house a collection of objects.

OBJECTS OF DESIRE

TOP ROW LEFT TO RIGHT

Floating shelves, such as these taupe-lacquered ones in my old dining room, are a great place for displays that can be refreshed every few months when inspiration strikes. Here, ceramics, rock crystal, Buddhas, books, and black-and-white photographs are united by their toning shades of black, white, and taupe. In between a pair of Baltus chairs with black-lacquered ball frames, timber occasional tables with a panel of rivets by Kelly Hoppen provide a good place to display glass bowls of hydrangeas. Propping up pictures is an easy way to add height to a display and means you can move them around at whim. The elegant curves of the Albedo table lamp by Lahumière Design are a counterpoint to the lines of the shelf and frames. Organic crystals bring great, positive energy to a space.

CENTER ROW LEFT TO RIGHT

Quirky elements add a note of surprise, like this vintage bronze lizard perching on a bronze Ajoure side table by Christian Liaigre, in front of a row of propped-up black-and-white photographs.
A simple display of matte white porcelain vessels of different sizes on a sleek black oak shelf is soothing to the eye.
A nicely balanced collection of black and white vessels of various shapes and sizes stands out against the backdrop of the subtly self-striped white curtain.

BOTTOM ROW LEFT TO RIGHT

The neat alignment of the black-and-white photograph by Ralph Gibson, stack of antique silver boxes, and Plexiglass container with coils of iris leaves makes a pleasing still life.
An alcove in an entrance lobby has become the perfect home for three organically shaped pots planted with orchids, the rough clay of the pots acting as a textural foil to the marble floor with its runner of black-dyed basalt.
Niches are the perfect place to create theatrical effects. In a bathroom, a vintage bronze figurine and a row of white ceramic books are dramatically lit against the backdrop of the beautiful polished plaster wall finish.

MOOD MAKERS

SENSES

For a home to feel comfortable and welcoming, all the senses need to be engaged by its design. Color, texture, form, lighting, scent, and sound all have a direct bearing on our mood, so it is important to determine what kind of atmosphere you want to create in each space before you decide on the specifics of decor and furnishings. Think about how and when each room is going to be used, for what activities, and by whom. All these aspects will come into play when you are designing your layout and making choices about surfaces, furniture, and accessories.

The combination of materials you choose and the ways and proportions in which they are applied set the mood of a room like nothing else. I always make up a detailed room board that shows not only the selection of surfaces, finishes, and colors I intend to use, but also the furniture and furnishings, fabrics and trims. When you are considering your palette of materials for each space, think about how each feels to the touch—how cocooning the upholstery and soft furnishings, how tactile and sensuous your bed linen, and how the flooring will feel underfoot.

Scent is one of the most important mood-enhancing elements to consider. It is so evocative and comforting and is the first thing we notice when we walk through a door. Fresh flowers and scented candles are the obvious choices and I consider both to be necessities, rather than luxuries. Candles also have the added dimension of soft, flattering illumination.

It may seem counterintuitive when considering mood, but don't overlook technology. Music is one of the greatest mood-lifters, so installing a sound system that plays music wherever you want it in the house at the touch of a button is a great investment.

OPPOSITE

A shaggy black goatskin rug adds fabulous, sensuous texture underfoot and instantly lends the hard lines of the chrome and leather furniture a softer, warmer feel. This rich mix of glamorous materials is a tactile feast for the eyes and the fingers.

ORGANIC

Flowers, greenery, and other natural elements add a sense of integrity to interiors, providing an essential layer of texture, color, and scent that contributes to the overall mood. I like to tailor the choice of flower or foliage to the setting in question—a grand hallway demands something bold and architectural, such as towering stems of arum lilies or a row of potted olive trees, while a small, scented bouquet is more fitting for a nightstand or bathroom. Repetition is key—I always use flowers in a single color, chosen to tie in with an accent used elsewhere in the scheme. Often a simple bowl of succulents on a bed of moss is all that's required, but displays of fruit or vegetables can be equally effective.

ABOVE LEFT

With their delicate blooms and curving stems, orchids have an unparalleled exotic beauty. Here, their sculptural form is accentuated by the glamorous backdrop of the textured wallpaper.

ABOVE RIGHT

You don't have to splash out to make a botanical impact in your home. Snake grass has been cut to uniform lengths and packed vertically into a wenge box, forming a minimalist, contemporary display.

ABOVE

Other natural elements to bring into your home include pebbles, crystal, coral, and driftwood. This display of Kate Hume's freeform glass vases, inspired by pebbles, introduces organic shapes and interesting reflections.

OPPOSITE

Green is the accent color in this moody, dramatically lit kitchen, introduced by three moss balls on the backlit floating shelves and cookie sheets filled with frondy grasses on the dark wood work surface.

MOOD MAKERS

SPIRITUAL

Whatever your beliefs, the spirit and energy of your home are important to your general sense of well-being. I am a great believer in the Eastern practice of feng shui, which works on the premise that everything—including us and our homes—is composed of energy. If that energy is not able to flow freely, it will have a negative impact on our productivity and happiness. The obvious culprit is clutter, so incorporating adequate and appropriate storage for your belongings into your interior goes a long way toward combatting this. I also like to surround myself with energy-enhancing elements such as natural crystals, fresh flowers, resin or farmed coral, Buddhas, and soothing music. I think of these things as a kind of acupuncture for the home.

OPPOSITE ABOVE LEFT

I have frequently incorporated Buddhas into my designs over the years, as I find them to be an incredibly calming and powerfully inspiring presence. This example, from Fiona Jordan, sits against the rustic backdrop of a wood-clad chalet wall.

OPPOSITE BELOW RIGHT

Floating rose heads in a half-full vase is an interesting, contemporary way to display flowers. The fragility of the petals contained within the clear glass plays against the strict lines of the wooden screen behind.

ABOVE

The delicate-looking but rock-hard branches of resin coral, from kellyhoppen.com, add rough, organic texture to a pale wood console table.

RIGHT

On this console table, the branching forms of coral are offset by the curves of the clear glass cloches of the anthropological display domes, with single stems of arum lilies adding height.

THE

EDIT

MAKE AN ENTRANCE

You have only one chance to make a good first impression, and nowhere more so than at home. Creating a wonderful entrance is as much about welcoming yourself home with the interiors equivalent of a big hug, as it is about setting

MAKE AN ENTRANCE

WELCOME

The front door and entrance hall create the first impressions of your home and set the tone for the rest of the house. Materials, colors, lighting, furniture, and accessories can all be used to create very different moods, from glamorous to cocooning, but the crucial thing is to make the space feel inviting. What greets you visually as you open the door is important, so consider introducing a focal point, such as art or statement lighting, and a console table or shelves for display, which will balance the vertical lines of the doorways. The design of the entrance hall should always be considered in conjunction with adjacent rooms and corridors, so that nothing jars or is out of kilter. Floor runners that lead you onward to other rooms also enhance the welcoming vibe.

PREVIOUS PAGE

I wanted my entrance hall to be dramatic, solid, and sharp, with a real wow factor. Using the grid, I designed the geometric black-and-white marble floor and accentuated the ceiling height with a Japanese-style runner, pivoting lacquered-wood shutters, a panel of specialist plaster, and a trio of pendant lights by Hervé Langlais for Galerie Negropontes, which hang directly above the bespoke table with its bronze base by Matt Stanwix. My photograph of Marilyn Monroe strikes the perfect note of glamour.

OPPOSITE

Decorated in soft taupe shades, this entrance hall is the epitome of quiet elegance. A beautiful Promemoria linen sofa with velvet pillows, silk Fortuny Scheherazade ceiling lights, and a custom-made chandelier by OCHRE cascading through the wrought-iron and wood staircase, carpeted in plush silk, create an inviting space that says, "Come in, sit down."

ABOVE

A wonderfully glamorous monochrome entrance hall, in Calacatta marble, polished white-waxed plaster, black wood paneling, and brass trim, with brass-framed panels of rose-gold mirror creating reflections and illusions.

Well-considered lighting is essential on stairs for both practical and aesthetic reasons. Safety is obviously of paramount concern but clever lighting will also accentuate the effect of whatever surfaces and finishes are at play, as well as adding to the drama of the whole effect by highlighting the sweeping curves or bold lines of the design. One of my favorite tricks is to suspend statement pendant lights that are works of art in their own right at different levels through the central well of a staircase—spirals or cascades of Swarovski crystals, clusters of glass globes, oversized lanterns, modern sculptural designs, or elaborate chandeliers.

OPPOSITE

The clean lines of this modern staircase in a polished white-waxed plaster finish, which contrasts sharply with the dark wood floor and door, are dramatically offset by the spectacular Swarovski crystal light. This spirals its way through all three stories of the house, ending just above the angular white-lacquered console table by Megaron that complements the sleek design.

THIS PAGE

This extraordinary sweeping staircase of wood and glass leads the eye up, while the black floor runner guides the way to the heart of the house. The chainmail Terzani light is hung low in the corner to bring focus and texture to this area. The cluster of vessels on the lacquer table and the leather bench that echoes the line of the stairs also add further layers of texture to the space.

LIVING SPACES

Living rooms are the workhorses of the modern home, often accommodating study, rest, and play. They can be private family spaces or more formal—and public—entertaining zones, and are frequently both. But whatever function they perform, they must always ooze comfort and conviviality.

THE EDIT

CIRCULATION

At the start of any project, when I go into a house, I think about how I feel in it. Spaces speak for themselves, and in a sense you need to tune in to this and have a conversation with each room, shake hands, and say, "We're in this together." This approach helps me to come up with a design that is appropriate for the building and that feels "right."

Large spaces are difficult to design, but also very exciting because the possibilities are endless. The first task is to assess the structure of the building, the architectural features, and the levels of natural light, and then figure out whether you need to make any alterations and how you are going to zone the space.

Particularly important in large or open-plan interiors, zoning defines different areas according to changes of function or mood by the style and arrangement of furniture and lighting, and often by the choices of materials and decor, too. The grid, which forms the structural "bones" of a design upon which all other layers of decoration and furnishing are built, plays a key role in this. Flow encompasses both the practicalities of how you move around a space and the things you see and the way you feel as you do so. It is the "air" that allows the room to breathe. Considered together, these concepts inform where furniture, art, and objects should be placed in order to create a harmonious interior.

PREVIOUS PAGE

My living area occupies a third of the large, open-plan, first-floor space of a former auction house. It runs from the entrance to the study, with a long marble ledge for displaying art and other treasures linking the spaces together. Two of the monumental wood-clad structural columns that punctuate the space create a natural sense of division from the dining area and kitchen, and this is underlined further by the linear style of the furniture. The combination of neutral tones, a rich palette of textures and materials, and dramatic lighting, including the sculptural Ribot floor lamp by De Castelli, add up to a warm, elegant living space.

RIGHT

This enormous room is part of an old school building, which I designed to create lots of different zones and sitting areas under the soaring ceiling rafters. The scheme comprises the perfect combination of furniture from different eras, fabrics, and textures, and the result is warm and comfortable, with a great sense of flow from the functional kitchen at the far end, through the informal eating area, to the sitting room, and formal dining space (out of shot). The view is great from any direction and there is always something of interest to catch the eye.

THIS PAGE AND OPPOSITE
The challenge with double-height spaces is that tall ceilings draw the eye upward, so you need to bring the focus back to the level where you live. This has been achieved here by the trio of Arteinmotion pendant lights hung at varying heights, the backlit bookcases built into the specialist-plaster walls, and the deep, contrasting bands of velvet on the floor-to-ceiling drapes.

LIVING SPACES

LEFT

The design of my previous living room was inspired by glamorous black-and-white photography, with dramatic ebony-stained floorboards and a black glass fireplace wall contrasting with the white-waxed plaster walls and white linen curtains with slim black runners. Black-and-white photographs—my treasured portrait of Marilyn Monroe and *Jessica in Lace Dress* by Louise Bobbe—adorned the walls. The centerpiece was the triangular vintage polished steel and brass coffee table around which the vintage chairs and Modénature sofas upholstered in bespoke damask covers were arranged, together with my signature Christian Liaigre pieces—the lacquer Flibuste Pedestal and bronze Ajoure side tables.

ABOVE

L-shaped rooms can be quite tricky to design, as you are in danger of ending up with a space that doesn't get used. Here, at the other end of my living room, which had French windows opening onto a balcony, I created another seating area in the same style, centered on the fabulous culled zebra rug that linked the two ends of the room together. Natural light flooded through the French windows during the day, and at night the Mark Brazier-Jones Sera floor lamp created atmospheric shadows.

THE EDIT

LIVING SPACES

HIGH DRAMA

Creating a sense of theater is essential in any living space. Some rooms have an intrinsic impact due to their sheer scale, or because of architectural features, such as a vast picture window with an incredible view, or decorative period moldings on the ceiling. If this is the case, these elements need to be made the most of and, to a certain extent, inform the mood of the room and the decor, furniture layout, and style of furnishings. In other spaces, you need to add the wow factor, whether that's with the use of a special, luxury material, a stunning artwork, sculpture, or antique, or a statement piece of furniture or lighting.

Playing with scale, symmetry, and balance is essential when it comes to creating drama and introducing an element of surprise. As ever, the grid comes to the fore, because emphasizing the vertical and horizontal planes is a great way to impose a sense of order and enhance the proportions of a room. This is especially key within a large open-plan and multifunctional living space, where the grid is fundamental in defining different zones. Creating interesting vistas and using focal points to draw the eye from one area to another will enhance the sense of vitality and energy within a space.

Lighting is another way to add drama. A carefully chosen statement light, whether it's a design classic, an oversized pendant, a crystal chandelier, or a contemporary sculptural piece, can have almost as much impact unlit as lit. At the same time, subtle lighting effects, such as wall or floor washes, shadow-gap lighting, or directional spotlights, can be used to highlight objects or surfaces and create theatrical pools of light and shadow.

LEFT

Gridlines galore! A view from the mezzanine walkway into my double-height living space clearly shows the use of the grid in the way the layout has been planned. The two structural support columns provide a natural point of division between the dining space and the main seating area, and all the furniture, lighting, surfaces, and finishes have been chosen and positioned with both the scale of the room and its horizontal and vertical lines in mind. When designing a vast space such as this, you have to consider not only how it is going to be used but also how it will look from every angle, to integrate it into the home as a whole. Here, you can look down at the space and still feel very much a part of it.

LIVING SPACES

OPPOSITE

This apartment is in an incredibly tall building and has large windows giving stunning views of the Beijing skyline and flooding the interior with amazing light. You almost feel as though you are in a glass box in the clouds, so I wanted to use a palette of gray, silver, and white tones to reflect the sky and make the space feel creative and warm. The stunning custom-made pendant light of free-blown glass by Dale Chihuly has an ethereal feel and is a star piece in the room—the perfect foil for the straight lines of the Christian Liaigre Augustin sofa and JNL Samara coffee table displaying glass bowls by Anna Torfs. The Robert Kuo floor lamps and pair of large DK Home vases create balance.

ABOVE

This sculptural staircase and hallway are the core of this home, and I designed the six French-style paneled doors of beveled glass to borrow light and views from the dining room beyond. The room itself appears like art, but the doors can be pivoted open to create one large, stunning space for entertaining.

LIVING SPACES

OPPOSITE

The sculptural curves of an original Arts and Crafts staircase, reminiscent of whipped cream, is complemented by a glass-topped coffee table alongside a modern white sofa, and a pair of vintage chairs, made edgy with black leather upholstery, studs, and a Fortuny pillow, with a bronze side table from Asiatides. This bold juxtaposition creates a wonderful and unexpected play of styles, materials, and textures.

ABOVE

In this comfortable living room in a Shenzhen apartment, which has stunning views through the floor-to-ceiling windows, the sofas, in taupe and cream linen and taupe smooth leather, are arranged around a pair of dark wood coffee tables by Casamilano. The walls have been clad with panels of luxury Arabascato marble, with a television screen set into one. These are balanced with bespoke units housing art and accessories behind a taupe wood grid facade that creates a sense of intrigue. Marble ledges for display emphasize the horizontal lines and are balanced by the vertical lines of the Holly Hunt pendant lights and floor lamp.

THE EDIT

CONNECTION

The living areas of your home need to function as public spaces to entertain friends and hold parties, and also as private spaces in which to relax, chat, read, and watch television. Large, open-plan spaces can incorporate more than one area that you might use in different ways or for different purposes. But while the materials, furniture, furnishings, and lighting with which you choose to decorate each zone don't need to be identical, they do need to share the same dialogue so that they work in harmony together and the overall space is balanced and coherent.

With the framework of the grid in mind, the prospect of creating separate zones within a large, open space is not overwhelming, as it soon becomes clear where a seating area should be, for example, and how the furniture and lighting within that grouping should be positioned. The lines of the grid are further defined when a space is divided up, either by the placement of a physical structure—such as a decorative screen, sliding doors, shelving unit, or large piece of furniture—or with a change of surface underfoot, or perhaps a combination of both.

Lighting can also be employed to mark out zones within the framework of the grid. A line of floor washers running along the base of a wall; a grid of recessed downlights in the ceiling; LED strips concealed along the top of cabinetry or the underside of shelves; a row of pendant lights suspended over a kitchen countertop or dining table; or the strict, balanced placement of floor or table lamps to create symmetry all provide a combination of ambient, task, and decorative or statement lighting.

RIGHT

The first feeling I had on walking into this extraordinary room was, "Wow! There is so much space," and the more I designed, the bigger it seemed to get. There are three main seating areas and two further intimate ones, all designed in the same palette and with threads of continuity running through them in terms of style, color, and texture. Each zone is connected by the underfoot grid, which comprises a central wide runner of white-lacquered timber, with walkways of natural wood on either side. The zones are punctuated by lacquer-topped tables with fluted, silver-plated copper bases displaying orchids in a collection of ceramic vessels. The perimeter of the central seating area, shown here, is demarcated by a pair of Galion console tables by Christian Liaigre behind each sofa, and four large white-bronze Robert Kuo floor lamps in each corner. The use of white here makes you feel as though you are floating in the sky.

OPPOSITE

The wonderful nuances of the textures and tones at play are evident here, in what appears at first glance to be a very simple palette. Warm natural wood, glossy lacquer, a combination of metallics, different tones of linen, silk, glass, and ceramics all combine to create a feeling of serene luxury. There are so many different textures, it almost makes the mouth water.

ABOVE

The central part of the room has been designed so that one half is almost a mirror image of the other, with the placement of floor lamps, ottomans, and ornamental vessels all echoing each other on either side of the central column, but with subtle differences in the secondary seating areas, such as round coffee tables instead of square, and different accessories on display. The symmetry of the main seating area in the foreground is obvious in the arrangement of the pair of sofas facing each other over two black-stained wood coffee tables with inset metallic runners. Working out the space planning and furniture layout on plan is essential in a large space such as this.

RIGHT

The structural columns that punctuate the space have been transformed into key features by cladding them with glossy white-lacquered wood and incorporating chrome-edged niches for the display of collections of glassware and ceramics.

THE EDIT

ABOVE

I love our study, which is like a collector's room housing the history of the old auction house, as well as inspiring books, art, and objects. It is furnished with vintage, modern, and classic pieces, such as the Cassina LC1 armchair by Le Corbusier, the Barbuda armchairs and coffee table by Christian Liaigre, the desk from kellyhoppen.com, and lights by Kevin Reilly. The zebra rug and bursts of orange enliven the neutral palette.

LIVING SPACES

CONCENTRATION

Working at home for some or all of the time is increasingly an inevitability of flexible modern living, and having a separate room in which to do it is essential in order to establish a separation between working and home life. Even if you don't work from home, having a dedicated space for dealing with household paperwork, catching up with social media, pursuing crafts or hobbies, or just indulging in reading or creative thinking away from the rest of the family is the ultimate luxury.

A home office or private study should be an inspiring, personal, and welcoming space that will allow your thoughts and creativity to run free, but also enable you to focus on the task at hand without too many distractions. The decor should be soothing but stimulating, with objects, artworks, and photographs that please and inspire you on show.

The key pieces of furniture and the focal points of the room are a large desk and comfortable chair, which should be placed in the center of the room, rather than tucked apologetically against a wall. Good lighting and adequate storage for paperwork, books, stationery, and other supplies are also essential. Bespoke joinery comes into its own in a home office, as it can be used to conceal technology and unsightly equipment from view, while cabinets and shelves may be designed specifically to accommodate whatever you need to store or display.

ABOVE

In this home office I created a minimalist environment that suited the client—a place where there are few distractions and the mind can focus. The simple lines of the Christian Liaigre desk and chair, and a second chair from Modénature, are completely in keeping with the spare mood of the room, where bonsai trees and other objects on custom-made bronze and wood shelving have been lit like works of art.

HEART
OF THE
HOME

All of life plays out in the kitchen, for this is truly the beating heart and social hub of the contemporary home. Here we fill our bellies as well as chill and chat—"earthing" ourselves, our family, and our friends, before embarking on the theater of our everyday lives.

THE EDIT

COMMUNICATION

PREVIOUS PAGE

This kitchen, in a previous home, was situated at one end of the large open-plan living area, so its design needed to be sympathetic to the space as a whole. The dark wood cabinets echo the wood used elsewhere in the space, and the black parquet flooring extends throughout, although softened with a silk rug in the living area. Chainmail curtains were hung at all the windows to help create a positive flow of energy. The cooktop is set into a stainless-steel counter at right angles to the main work surface, creating a working area on one side and a breakfast bar on the other (see also pages 272–73).

The kitchen is nearly always the first room you go to as soon as you arrive home and it's the room that everyone naturally gravitates to. As the central hub—for cooking, eating, chatting, family life, and so much more besides—its successful design is crucial to a happy home. Being clear and realistic about your requirements is the first step to achieving this. Are you a great cook and love entertaining or do you just need somewhere to throw easy suppers together? Do you require any special equipment—a coffee machine, juicer, boiling-water faucet, or audio-visual system?

HEART OF THE HOME

OPPOSITE

This family dining or homework area in the corner of a kitchen has a wonderfully cocooning feel, thanks to the semicircular seating that envelops people around the table. The artwork by Jean Baptiste Huynh is the focal point, while the Kevin Reilly light echoes the circular Modénature table below it.

BELOW

A refreshing mix of materials has been juxtaposed in this monochrome kitchen. The linear elements—the white-lacquered units and island, white-painted oak table from St Paul Home, Kevin Reilly Altar light, dark oak door and floor—are offset by Andrew Martin's acrylic Saturn chairs, which seem to float, the round glass vases, Hive task lights, and playful mirrors.

Do you need to accommodate small children, a quiet corner for homework, or pets? Is there space for a dining table, breakfast bar, sofa, separate utility area, or all of the above?

Practicality is everything in a kitchen, so ensure that there is a good ergonomic flow between your key areas of refrigerator, sink, and stove. Make sure there is sufficient free work surface for preparing food, loading and unloading the dishwasher, taking hot things out of the oven, and so on, and think about your route to and from the table.

Consider the suitability and maintenance of materials carefully—work surfaces, sinks, and floors should all be easy to clean and able to withstand a certain amount of wear and tear without becoming scratched or stained.

Designing a kitchen is a bit like doing a very complicated jigsaw puzzle and I always work with a specialist kitchen designer to ensure that my clients get exactly the right layout and combination of storage, display, gadgets, and furniture to fit their particular requirements.

THE EDIT

BELOW

This is one of my favorite kitchens I've ever had (see also page 269). When I bought the apartment, I relocated the kitchen from another room, which then became my gym; I wanted to incorporate it into the main living space as it's such a pivotal part of the modern home. People would always gather there and I could never get rid of them.

OPPOSITE

The adjoining dining area was a great space for conversation, for informal meals, and working on the computer. The dark wood table and white leather chairs, both from Modénature, fit with the theme of the room as a whole and offset the lines and angles of the kitchen design. I had the circular chainmail light specially made by OCHRE to tie in with the chainmail hanging at the windows.

HEART OF THE HOME

OPPOSITE

The informal eating area in a corner of the kitchen in my new home has built-in banquette seating and chairs around a taupe-lacquered table, with backlit shelves behind displaying an array of ceramic vases, coral, and other objects. It is located at one end of the working part of the kitchen, so people can sit, chat, or watch television while I prepare the food. It's also a lovely, cozy space in which to eat.

ABOVE

The design of the wall-mounted kitchen units echoes the structural columns that frame the space and emphasize the grid. The marble breakfast bar ensures that the space feels both inclusive and partially enclosed, while also reflecting the horizontal lines of the extensive formal dining table in front and the dramatic pendant light suspended over it. The use of Cararra marble for the backsplash and counter gives a luxurious feel that suits the tone of the room as a whole.

THE EDIT

RIGHT AND BELOW

The simply furnished dining area (below) is at one end of the large, teak-style resin and quartz Poggenpohl kitchen (right), which has three walls of built-in cabinets and wall-mounted units, as well as two large islands, with a cooktop in one and one of two sinks in the other. The family that live here have lots of children, so the round table and eight tub chairs, upholstered in glazed linen, encourage everyone to gather together. The overscaled Avico light by Fontana Arte gives the seating area prominence, creating the feeling that this is a space where you sit and enjoy yourself. The collection of ceramic vessels is from Absolute Flowers.

HEART OF THE HOME

LEFT

How you set the table evokes the type of evening you're going to have. Neutral shades of taupe, stone, and pearly gray with milky blue glass on a calico cloth create a cool, relaxed vibe, with pleated napkins and organic spheres offsetting the order of the place settings. Coral and twigs on the mantelpiece play against the silver wallpaper runner.

BELOW

This chic dining area is separated from the kitchen on the right by a counter (not seen) and from the living area on the left by an open partition that beautifully frames two huge DK Home vases. The bronze-based wood table and velvet and leather chairs from Promemoria give a luxe, glamorous feel to the space, along with the Mark Brazier-Jones Libertine chandelier and the end wall of marble, with wooden shelves displaying glassware and vases.

LEFT AND BELOW

This linear SieMatic kitchen is made light, bright, and fresh by the predominant use of white, stainless steel, chrome, and glass, but with blackened oak floorboards to ground the space and create drama. White is one of the happiest colors you can use, but mixing it with something darker and creating contrast makes it even more effective. Runners of white poured resin inset into the flooring define the grid and help to line everything up, including the row of Danetti bar stools, giving a sense of flow between the kitchen and dining zone in front of the window. Low-level lighting at the base of the units enhances this effect, while downlights under the wall-mounted cabinets provide task lighting for the work surface.

OPPOSITE ABOVE LEFT

A big refrigerator is essential in my view. Here, I had my Sub-Zero refrigerator and oven built into bespoke dark wood cabinets to tie in with the blackened parquet flooring and other low-level kitchen units (see also pages 269 and 272–73).

OPPOSITE ABOVE RIGHT

This island unit with cabinets on one side and bar stools on the other is part of a collection I designed for Smallbone. In this bright, airy corner, and with two pendant lights hanging over the shiny marble surface, it makes a great alternative place to chat, eat, or work on the computer.

LEFT

In a space where hard materials reign, a cream leather bar stool with cool chrome edging adds a touch of luxe softness, especially when juxtaposed with the shiny surface of a milk-glass countertop.

OVERLEAF LEFT

The faucets, furniture, and lighting you choose are your pieces of kitchen sculpture. This kitchen bar is a welcoming and attractive place to sit on comfortable cream leather chairs facing the working area of the Boffi kitchen. There is also a conventional table and chairs behind for a more formal dining experience in this large, inclusive family kitchen (see also pages 284–85).

OVERLEAF RIGHT

Located at one end of a kitchen, this chic dining space—a favorite of mine—is the main dining area in the house and is given due prominence by the choice of luxury material for the table and the nickel-framed fireplace set high into the wall like a piece of art. The design of the table, made from beautiful slabs of marble, was based on a simple console table. Cream leather and nickel chairs and the row of slim, cylindrical glass pendants complete the understated glamour of the space.

THE EDIT

CONVERSATION

The place where you fill your belly should be a happy one, whether you can cook or not. Dining spaces need to be inviting and comfortable, encouraging people to linger and savor the company and conversation as much as the food and wine you serve. Whether you have a large open-plan kitchen with an inclusive, informal eating area, or a separate formal dining room—these days, frequently considered a luxury and overlooked in favor of a study, playroom, or extra bedroom—the dining area is somewhere to gather friends and family, celebrate special occasions, and make lasting memories.

In terms of style, if your kitchen and dining area open onto other spaces, the colors and materials you choose should reflect those in the adjoining areas so there is a sense of continuity. If the dining area is in a separate room, you can feel free to create a different, more opulent mood with a palette of materials, textures, and colors that come into their own by candlelight.

Flexible lighting is key for kitchens and dining spaces and should combine task, mood, and statement lights, controlled, as always, by dimmer switches. Lights above dining tables need to be positioned carefully so that the light they cast is practical, flattering, and comfortable for the eyes. Again, if the dining space and kitchen areas read as one, ensure that the lighting styles in the working and dining zones are sympathetic to one another in terms of materials, and balance each other in terms of shape and proportions. It's a great opportunity to create arresting plays of textures and scale.

RIGHT

Perfect for entertaining, this imposing bar area was designed for clients in Shenzhen, using a palette of luxury materials including Calacatta marble, polished brass, rose-gold mirror, and taupe wood. Brass inlays have been used in the timber floor, marble bar, and mirrored panel on the wall behind. These runners wrap over onto the ceiling, giving a feeling of enclosure to the area. White silk and brass pendant lights are suspended over the marble bar top, where a selection of brass and marble accessories is displayed to complete the glamorous effect.

THE EDIT

BELOW AND OPPOSITE

The inviting dining area in this fantastic family kitchen has its own identity but is sympathetic to the style of the Boffi units behind, with their sleek configuration echoed by the strong lines of the oak table, which was stained on site to match the floorboards precisely. The sculptural curves and contrasting scale of the classic Wishbone chairs by Hans Wegner and the all-engulfing, velvet-upholstered Tom Dixon Wing chairs create a playful sense of balance. This almost comical contrast of scale is continued by the three enormous lacquered-steel Caravaggio pendant lights, with three circular containers of moss and succulents placed directly beneath them.

OVERLEAF

This light-filled dining room in the south of France is decorated in a calm palette of cream and white tones, with sand-colored matting anchoring the table on the terrazzo floor that was the starting point for the scheme. The contemporary white resin-plaster table is complemented by white leather chairs, whose dark wood legs, along with the sideboard, ground the scheme. The white rectangular pendant light defines the grid but seems to float ethereally over the tabletop. The only colors in the room are the moody blue and green tones in the artworks.

HEART OF THE HOME

OPPOSITE

The strict alignment of furniture using the grid is essential so that everything appears comfortable in its position and seems to belong there. In this open-plan, double-height space, the circular dining table has been placed directly in front of a specialist plaster wall that runs all the way to the ceiling between two windows. One of the spectacular Arteinmotion lights—a chandelier within a metal gimbal—that hang throughout the space at different heights is suspended directly above the center of the table.

ABOVE

This view, like a cross section cut through a 3-D plan of the property, with little pockets of the upstairs visible, shows how important it is that all the materials and furnishings work together so that the vista is harmonious from any direction. The furniture, upholstery, pillows, and tables in the formal living space in the foreground, the dining area beyond it, and the television corner to the left of the space are all different, but the shapes, tones, and textures work together and are unified by the flooring and joinery.

HEART OF THE HOME

Different views of my dining space show how everything relates to something else and there is always another surprise for the eye—the mark of a good design is that you see something new every time you look. The dining space is defined by the long stone table that I designed for the space and which seats up to 30 people on a mix of Velin chairs and banquettes by Christian Liaigre, benches by Guillaume Alan, and stools by Tom Dixon.

OPPOSITE ABOVE LEFT

This view down the length of the table, through the pivoting lacquered doors into the television room, with the kitchen on the left (see also pages 206–07 and 274–75), clearly shows the grid lines. The framework that I created between the structural columns is evident, and the spectacular pendant light cuts through the mid-height.

OPPOSITE ABOVE RIGHT

Seen from upstairs, the dining table takes center stage in the space to the left of the support columns that zone off the living area (see also pages 248 and 256–7).

OPPOSITE BELOW

Views of the dining area are framed by the open pivoting doors of the television room, with its informal seating; the room can be closed off for watching movies in seclusion.

LEFT

The table aligns with the black custom plaster runner, while the sharp diagonal of the staircase seems to cut through the Japanese-inspired slatted panel on the wall behind it. The gold plinth displaying the sculpture by Paul Vanstone and the stone pots under the stairs create balance.

THE EDIT

RIGHT

Looking from the kitchen through to the conservatory and balcony, the black poured-resin floor of the chic, high-spec kitchen gives way to black narrow wooden floorboards. The furniture is a mix of custom-made designs and classic pieces, such as the Christian Liaigre stool and Warren Platner Knoll chair with purple leather upholstery.

BELOW

Drama is brought to the glossy white Boffi kitchen cabinets by the black granite countertops and backsplashes. The crisp black doorway frames the view into the dining room, where the narrow black floorboards resume again and black shutters filter the light.

OPPOSITE

In this Georgian townhouse with a contemporary twist, the dining space leads into the kitchen, which in turn leads into the conservatory; all the spaces have different purposes but need to have a visual link so that one flows seamlessly into the next. The simple monochrome palette, with accents of pale pink, purple, and bronze, including the hare sculpture by Barry Flanagan, works perfectly. The dark wood B&B Italia dining table is surrounded by dark wood and white leather Christian Liaigre chairs. The decorative glass-paneled doors were custom-made for the space, and the antique chandelier is the client's own.

BATH ROOMS

In Japan, bathing is a revered and ancient tradition, and the bathroom, accordingly, assumes an important status. Thus, it is incredibly important to me to give what might previously have been considered a mundane room a sense of ceremony and sublime comfort through the use of fine materials and textures.

PREVIOUS PAGE
Soft lighting and reflective surfaces are a great combination for a relaxing atmosphere. In one of my old bathrooms, the Bette Starlet bathtub was set into a milk-glass surround, with KH2 faucets that I designed for Waterfront mounted on a backlit marble panel. Blush-pink roses and a scented candle set the feminine tone.

THIS PAGE
A cool white Thassos marble bathroom is enlivened by the organic texture of a runner of pebbles set in resin, which runs up facing walls and along the floor in-between. Glass vases of farmed coral add further layers of organic form and texture.

CLEAN

Bathrooms are very much private spaces in which to refresh and relax. They need to be practical rooms, but it is so easy to create something different. The bathtub, sink, and faucets are the sculptures of a bathroom, and the lighting and textures are the main design tools. I line up everything on the grid, which I define with two contrasting materials—stone with wood, marble, or milk glass, for instance. The third essential material is mirror, which adds glamour and bounces light and reflections around the room. The objects and elements you choose to display can be used to change the mood from feminine to masculine.

THIS PAGE
Sheer opulence with a view. This sensational bathroom was designed using Calacatta marble for the walls and floor, with inlays, borders, and details in polished brass, and a custom-made Corian sink and storage unit. Spectacular views can be enjoyed from the Harmony bathtub, which is part of the collection I designed for Apaiser.

OPPOSITE ABOVE LEFT AND BELOW LEFT

In this stunning bathroom, I used luxurious Carrara marble for both the walls and floor. The grid is defined by the niche over the toilet, the elongated mirror above the sink, and the floating shelves. The inverted L-shaped sink creates geometric interest and reflects the design of the bathtub with its graphic black panel.

OPPOSITE ABOVE RIGHT

The open latticework design of this black sink with a block faucet, both from Toscoquattro, adds great textural detail to a simple design.

OPPOSITE BELOW RIGHT

The square sink and chunky, blackened wood shelves appear to float over the white stone runner set into the black timber floor.

RIGHT

This fantastic, extra-deep sink has great presence, set on a blackened oak washstand positioned on the central runner of the same wood set into the taupe milk-glass floor. The elegant curve of the sculptural faucet from my collection is a foil to the straight lines.

BELOW RIGHT

The expanse of Calacatta Oro marble on the walls and floor is broken up by runners of mirror above the white Corian vanity ledge and the opaque-glass door to the toilet cubicle. The taupe-stained oak storage unit injects warmth into the glamorous scheme.

BELOW

Water runs through the cut-out organic shapes in the surface of this unusual stone sink, introducing textural interest and soft curves to counteract the sharp lines of the design.

RELAXATION

My optimum bathroom layout includes a statement bathtub—the standout piece in the room, which ideally should take center stage—two sinks, a shower, and a toilet, as well as sufficient storage space. Interesting plays of materials with contrasting textures and finishes can create wonderful effects, with imaginatively designed lighting enhancing the characteristics of each. Bathroom lighting should include at least three circuits for a combination of general, ambient, and task lighting over the sink, all controlled by dimmers or a pre-programmed system for creating different moods at the flick of a switch.

THIS PAGE AND OPPOSITE

My master bathroom is probably my favorite of all time. The Harmony tub I designed, made from reclaimed marble, is part of my collection for Apaiser, and was inspired by lotus flowers and a series of bowls I designed many years ago for Wedgwood, which made this incredible pattern when stacked. For extra presence, I set the bathtub in the center of the taupe wood floor on a Calacatta marble plinth, lit from underneath, to create a floating effect, and also from above, by Niamh Barry's amazing loop light, which reflects and highlights its sculptural form. A runner of the same marble is used behind the glass shower cubicle to give it presence.

THIS PAGE

The Origami floor-standing sink (left) and bathtub (top), designed by me for Apaiser, are the star pieces of one of my bathrooms. The walls are clad in beautiful gray-veined marble with panels of shiny black lacquer, one of which conceals a closet, while gray-toned wood flooring adds warmth. In another of my bathrooms (above and top left), marble also clads the bathtub and floor, which is inset with a white resin runner.

THIS PAGE CLOCKWISE FROM RIGHT

Marble is a practical choice for bathrooms, providing natural patterning, color, and texture. Beautifully veined Arabescato stone is offset by gray plaster, ebonized wood, and white bathroom fixtures. The hues are echoed in the adjoining bedroom. Polished marble runners play against the other matte and glossy finishes that make up the textural palette.

LEFT

Being small rooms where no one spends any length of time, guest bathrooms are great spaces to make dramatic statements or to use unexpected materials. The seemingly old-fashioned gold-and-charcoal Botanic wallpaper that I designed for Graham & Brown looks distinctly contemporary, with the square stone sink set within a bespoke oxidized-metal vanity unit that fills the entire width of the narrow room. Dornbracht taps are mounted onto the mirror runner that reflects the pendant lights from Eicholtz.

RIGHT

In another narrow bathroom, in one of my previous houses, I had the carved, dark gray marble sink fitted wall to wall and exaggerated the slim proportions of the room with a runner of mirror and the incredible Gessi faucet that extends all the way from the ceiling to the sink. The polished plaster walls, moody lighting, and backlit niche create a great sense of drama.

OPPOSITE

The shimmery, dark mosaic tiles that clad the walls and bench in this steam room have been cleverly lit to create an atmospheric effect. The luxe gray marble flooring makes a chic combination.

BELOW

With its distinctive pattern and tones of blue-gray and taupe, Wavy Willow marble from Livra has been used to clad the walls, Duravit Daro bathtub, and vanity unit in this bathroom. Architectural lighting behind the mirror enhances the linear design statement.

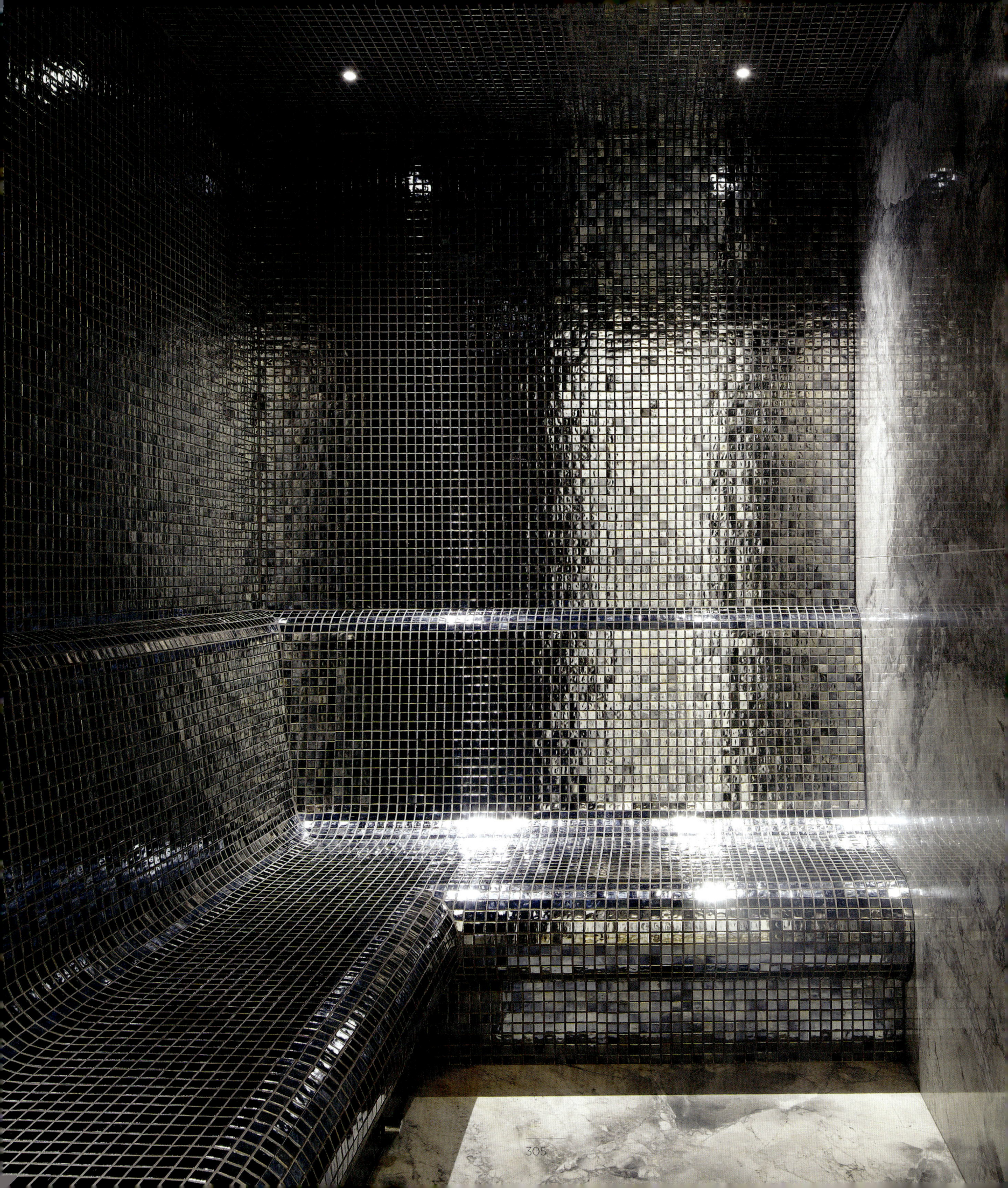

OPPOSITE ABOVE AND BELOW LEFT

The rich chocolate browns and taupes of the Eramosa stone walls give this bathroom a feeling of sumptuous luxury. The horizontal stripes are accentuated by the shutters I designed for Shutterly Fabulous, and by the sink and shelves, backed with marble to make a feature of them. The glass shower cubicle ensures nothing detracts from the statement stone.

OPPOSITE BELOW RIGHT

Panels of resin-coated wood create a cabin-like effect in this shower, with fixtures from Dornbracht. The lighting brings out the fabulous tones and textures of the grain while creating reflections on the shiny surface.

ABOVE

The cylindrical, floor-standing Corian sink is given importance by its position on the cream stone runner that cuts through the dark wood floor and continues up the wall in mirror, onto which the faucets are mounted. Lighting highlights the rough surface of the specialist plaster wall finish.

ABOVE RIGHT

The gentle pattern and coffee, cream, and taupe tones of this Jura gray honed limestone from Livra create a warm mood. Niches built into the wall above the toilet and bathtub create interest and depth, as well as providing a ledge to place candles.

RIGHT

The walls of this guest bathroom are a wonderful textural mix of Grigio Belemi stone and specialist plaster, with taupe-lacquered shutters and a mirror runner, while the floor is Grigio Belemi stone inset with taupe timber. The floor-standing sink is by Apaiser, with a faucet by Antonio Lupi.

OPPOSITE

This spectacular bathroom is bathed in a soft golden light from the backlit panels, which plays on the glossy surfaces of the brass runners and the horizontally veined marble, accentuating its warm tones of light and dark taupe. Intricate latticework brass panels create an alcove around the freestanding bathtub, screening off the toilet on one side and the shower on the other, while creating magical reflections.

ABOVE

The combination of the shimmering bronze specialist plaster wall finish, mirror, and glossy marble flooring inlaid with strips of brass creates an opulent effect in my guest bathroom. It is the perfect setting to display my gold-leaf Murano glass owl on the interlocking boxes of brass, mirror, and black anthracite designed by Kelly Hoppen Interiors. The cube-shaped sink, alongside my glamorous boxes with their reflective surfaces, follows suit.

ABOVE RIGHT

With only a subtle variance in color tone, a smooth, cream, limestone sink stands out in sharp relief against the herringbone texture of the specialist plaster wall finish.

RIGHT

Sinks can be like sculptural artworks. This egg-shaped floor-standing example was custom-made in the same glossy taupe stone as the walls and floor, with mirror and wood runners respectively. A simple ceiling-mounted faucet is both dramatic and unusual.

309

SLEEP SANCTUARY

Your bedroom is your private retreat
and personal recharging point.
It is where you start and finish every day, making it
one of the most important rooms in the home.
I love to use fabrics in abundance here, to create
a suitably luxurious, cosseting, and intimate cocoon

THE EDIT

DREAM

Unlike the public areas of the home, the master bedroom is all about you. This is a personal and private space that should make you feel safe, secure, relaxed, and happy. It is a room that needs to feel as good as it looks, with soft, sensuous, warm textures that feel great against the skin and under bare feet. Working with a soothing palette of gentle neutrals—based around tones of cream, taupe, and gray—will always result in a harmonious, calming space. Lighting is key to evoking different moods, with a flexible combination of task, mood, and statement lights, while layers of scent and flowers contribute to the sense of well-being.

PREVIOUS PAGE

A symmetrical bedroom is the most harmonious and conducive to rest. This cream, sand, and black room has been designed so that one half is almost a mirror image of the other, with the bed and picture above it being the central focus. An off-white rug on the glossy black floorboards anchors the room and is echoed in the framing of the artwork. The elegant curved chair legs break up the strict lines elsewhere, while the floor-standing vases of roses, echoed by the bouquets on the nightstands, add a balancing note of asymmetry.

ABOVE AND OPPOSITE

Texture is everything in my bedroom. Onto a foundation of taupe joinery and floorboards is layered a tactile mix of linen, velvet, and silk in soothing charcoal, taupe, and cream. The bed is the centerpiece, flanked by bespoke silk rugs, wall-mounted nightstands, backlit slatted runners, and clusters of OCHRE glass pendants. My lacquered Spencer Fung dressing table and stool, table lamp and damask bench by Christian Liaigre, photographs by Horst P Horst and Ellen von Unwerth, and vintage velvet chairs with Sé tables and linen screen, strike just the right notes of glamour and luxe.

THE EDIT

The bed is the most important piece of furniture and should have due prominence. Buy the largest and comfiest you can find, and dress it with top-quality cottons and linens—I prefer mine to be white. The mix of bedding is like a recipe that is part and parcel of the flavor and taste of a room. I start with the bedcover, which must be all encompassing and pool luxuriantly to the floor; I often have one for summer—in linen, cotton, or silk—and another for winter—in velvet, cashmere, or fur—and I sometimes add runners of contrasting textures. The headboard and base come next, which I usually upholster in the same fabric—linen, velvet, leather, or faux suede. Four to six pillows, with contrasting bands or buttons, add further layers of luxury and texture.

ABOVE AND OPPOSITE

A bedroom must look amazing from every angle, including when you are lying in bed. In my master bedroom, a large picture window gives spectacular views through to the double-height living space. The custom-made ledge beneath is perfect for storing books and displaying glass vases of roses, crystals, and other objects that I find pleasing to look at and that add the all-important layer of scent and feeling of well-being. The comfortable linen chaise longue is one of my designs and is a great place to relax and read under the gorgeous Hermès throw, with light from the sculptural vintage lamp on the shelf behind, which also highlights the photograph on the wall by Louise Dahl-Wolfe. The sculptural metal table by Vikram and Divya Goyal is a great accent piece and its organic flower-shaped form is a feminine counterpoint to the sharp lines of the joinery. The sumptuous velvet throws on the bed echo the lines of the damask bench by Christian Liaigre, and both emphasize the grid while adding further layers of texture to the palette.

SLEEP SANCTUARY

OPPOSITE

The glamorous pair of crystal chandeliers that hang on each side of this comfortable bed give it a sense of importance and create lovely patterns of light and shadows on the runners of taupe specialist plaster by Polidori Barbera on the wall behind them. The underlit dark wood bedside shelves echo the fabulous silver-paneled cabinet at the foot of the bed, which conceals the television. The shimmering silver and crystal, the gleaming dark wood, and the rich mix of cream fabrics on the bed are what give this simply furnished room a feeling of opulence.

ABOVE

This ultimate attic hideaway incorporates a Promemoria bed with Holly Hunt nightstands and a seating area, comprising a sofa and chairs by Meridiani facing each other over a bespoke leather ottoman, with a black copper and cream-lacquered Robert Kuo Drumstool and lamps by Porta Romana. With its angled ceiling, this space is deeply cocooning, with a sensuous mix of velvet, silk, and suede furnishings and a silk carpet.

SLEEP SANCTUARY

OPPOSITE ABOVE LEFT

The soft hues of bleached driftwood, beach pebbles, and shells have been combined with natural materials and a rich mix of textures—including wood, wicker, lacquer, cotton, linen, and velvet—to create this light, airy, beachside bedroom in Barbados. The large bell-shaped pendants by Gervasoni, Minottitalia circular mirror, Kelly Hoppen stool, and La Fibule armchair add organic shapes and curves.

OPPOSITE CENTER LEFT

The stylish lines of the Andrée Putman (for Ralph Pucci) sofa, upholstered in pale cream linen and with two perfectly proportioned pillows, make it the perfect, elegant piece for a bedroom.

OPPOSITE ABOVE RIGHT

Layers of textural detail are presented in the form of self-patterned cotton pillowcases, contrasting with a glamorous paneled headboard upholstered in eelskin, against a backdrop of specialist plaster.

OPPOSITE BELOW LEFT AND BELOW RIGHT

Two views of this bedroom with its textural taupe palette show how the various finishes play off one another to create a luxurious, warm, multi-toned effect. Reflected in the high-gloss lacquered mirror, the bed and sofa are both dressed with combinations of linen and crushed silk velvet. A linen Porta Romana bench contrasts with the sheen of the silk carpet and the netted sheers edged with crushed silk velvet and overlaid with linen drapes. The Jeremy Cole ceramic pendants highlight the leather-upholstered headboard and the specialist plaster on the wall behind.

ABOVE

This tranquil taupe bedroom with turquoise accents is pure East meets West, with my signature floating shelves and slatted panels, screens, and runners of taupe timber giving texture to the walls and ceiling. A feature wall behind the bed of silver-leaf wallpaper beautifully offsets the clients' fabulous artwork by Diane Tuft. The velvet runner and pillows take their color cue from the art, while the white leather bench and the taupe leather bed base and headboard play against the linen and velvet fabrics that dress the bed.

PREPARATION

A separate dressing room, or a dedicated dressing area within a bedroom, is a luxury that is well worth the investment. Keeping your bedroom free from clutter ensures the atmosphere remains calm and conducive to rest, and having a tailor-made storage system for all your clothes, shoes, and accessories makes getting ready a much easier process.

Dressing rooms are very personal spaces and how you design yours will depend on the items you need to accommodate and how you like to coordinate your clothing. The first step, therefore, is to consider all the garments you need to store—from ball gowns, to work suits, to underwear, activewear, ties, shoes, and purses—and decide whether they need to be hung, folded, rolled, or stacked.

Closet doors, whether conventionally opening, pivoting, or sliding, are the opportunity to introduce different surface textures, finishes, and fabulous handles. For a harmonious result, the materials and style should coordinate with the rest of the room or adjoining space. Good lighting and a full-length mirror or two are prerequisites, and some form of seating—a bench, chair, or ottoman—is useful.

OPPOSITE

A dressing room is the perfect location for a single statement chair, such as the classic Arne Jacobsen Swan.

ABOVE

This custom-made television, vanity, and storage unit, in high-gloss taupe lacquer with a slatted frame and trim in polished brass, is a stunning feature at one end of a guest bedroom. The Contardi hanging lights emphasize the grid and create symmetry, while a pair of velvet ottomans add softness as well as balance.

ABOVE RIGHT

A dressing table or desk, partially screened by rose-gold glass panels framed with polished brass, has been created with a custom-made floating ledge in black oak set against a wall panel of Calacatta marble with inset polished brass runners. The curved shape and linen upholstery of the swivel chair are a foil to the straight lines and hard materials that create drama and opulence.

RIGHT

This neatly ordered walk-in wardrobe, adjoining the master bedroom shown on page 319, features glass-fronted cabinets lit from within—total joy. The white-lacquered and smoked-glass units with sliding doors and gunmetal detailing from Poliform are perfectly complemented by the dark taupe wood floor.

ABOVE

A built-in dressing table beneath a window positioned between two long rows of beautifully grained oak veneer closets makes a great focal point and benefits from the natural light. Simple cut-out handles provide the only detail in this minimalist design.

ABOVE RIGHT AND RIGHT

Two views show that this generous-sized dressing room has bespoke storage for every item, including shoes, purses, and shirts. Dark-stained oak veneer has been used for the stylish combination of open and closed storage, with integral lighting and an island unit of drawers with a built-in, velvet-cushioned seat. Two large bronze-framed mirrors tone with the dark joinery and floorboards.

OPPOSITE ABOVE AND BELOW

My dressing room is my sanctuary and has the feel of a high-end atelier, with the pair of plush vintage chairs upholstered in pink-toned taupe velvet, glossy India Mahdavi stools, stunning pendant lights from Edition Limitée, and glamorous black-and-white photography, including a portrait of me by David Bailey, *Jessica in Lace Dress* by Louise Bobbe above the chairs, and my photograph of Jibby Beane by Nadav Kander on the opposite wall. All my shoes, purses, and clothes are housed on well-lit open racks, shelves, or rails, so I can see exactly where everything is, while other items are stored in bespoke drawers.

INDEX

Page numbers in *italic* refer to illustrations

A

Aarnio, Eero *129*
Abbot and Boyd *181*
Alan, Guillaume *290–1*
ALMA *59*
Amtico 27
Apaiser *297, 300–1, 302, 307*
Apparatus Studio *197*
aquamarine *194*, 195, *214*
architectural features 256–61
art collections 226–7, *265*, 267
Arteinmotion *211, 252–3, 288*
Arts and Crafts *260*
artwork 14, *24, 112, 132, 223, 232*, 245
Asian cultures 36–43
Asiatides *119, 260*
asymmetry *13, 41, 311*
Atollo *74*
Auer, Tristan *212*

B

B&B Italia *293*
backsplashes *275*
Bailey, David *323*
balance 14–25, 41, *148*, 228, 231, 257, *321*
Baltus *153, 232*
banners *see* runners
banquette seating *274*
Barry, Niamh *300*
bars *225, 282–3*
baseboards 50, *64*, 95
bathrooms 294–309
  guest bathrooms *114*, 165, *218, 233, 304, 307, 309*
  lighting *294*, 297, 300, *300–1, 304–8*
  moods 297, 300
  neutral color schemes *152*
  runners *62, 64, 65, 66–7, 114, 296, 300–1, 303, 304, 307, 308*
  screens *308*
  use of accent colors in *186, 189*
  use of marble in *107, 296*, 297, *297–305, 308*
bathtubs *294*, 297, 300, *302*
BD Design *69, 116*
Beane, Jibby *210, 323*
Beard, Peter *223*
Beau McClellan *122, 182, 208–9*
bedding 314
bedrooms 69, 310–23
  dark color schemes *164–5*, 165, *169, 170–1*
  fabrics 310
  flooring 102
  lighting 312, *312–13, 316, 318*
  mirrors *318*, 320
  neutral color schemes *151, 158–63*
  pillows 314
  texture in *166, 170–1, 312–13, 318*
  use of accent colors in *179, 181, 182, 187–91, 194*, 195, *196–7, 214*
beds: headboards *151, 153, 164, 169*
  neutral colors *151, 153, 158–9*
  pillows on *158–9, 164, 169*
  Promemoria design *317*
  runners *34, 194*, 314, *319*
  and texture *312*
Bellavista *208–9*
benches *221*, 312, *318*
Berger, Alison, for Holly Hunt *160*
Bleu Nature *126, 169*
blue accent colors 194–5
Bobbe, Louise *254, 323*
Bocci *181*
Boffi *280, 284, 292*
bookshelves *133, 182, 227*
Brazier-Jones, Mark:
  chair designs *188*
  lighting *87, 130–1, 255, 277*
breakfast bars *275*
Broom, Lee *107, 157*
Brown, Ralph *53*
Buddhas *238*

C

cabinetry 50, 52, *92–3*, 95
  display *177, 230*
  use of color in 176, *177, 178*, 183
candles 234, *294, 307*
Caravaggio *284–5*
carpets 102
Casamilano *261*
chainmail *141*
  curtains *117, 122, 269, 273*
  lighting *247, 273*
chair rails 50, 95
chairs *55*, 129, 139, *221*
  armchairs *154, 155, 214, 318*
  Christian Liaigre designs *169, 189, 266, 293*
  dining chairs *21, 271, 284–7*
  Kelly Hoppen designs *169, 196*
  statement chairs *320*
  transparent chairs *129, 134–5*
  use of accent color *174, 178*
  Warren Platner designs *192, 292*
chaise longue *167, 314–15*
chandeliers 116, 257
  in bedrooms *12, 160, 316*
  in dining areas *182, 211, 277, 288, 293*
  over staircases *80–1, 84, 85, 87, 130–1, 244*, 246
chest of drawers *105*
Chihuly, Dale *258*
Ciancimino 27
circulation 250–5
citrus colors 182–5, *266*
Clift, Robert *80*
Close, Glenn *168*
closets *55, 94, 100, 321*
  dressing room 320, *321, 322*
clutter 238
Cole, Jeremy *154, 165, 211, 219, 318*
color 234
  accent colors 174–99, *237, 266, 319*
  dark tones 164–71
  and displays 231
  Eastern interiors 41
  and fabrics *146–7*
  in kitchen and dining areas *180*, 282
  metallics 104–25, *264*
  monochrome *52–3, 68, 147*, 156, *174, 185*, 187, *196, 254–5, 292–3*
  neutrals *38–9*, 39, 148–71, 176, *248, 264*, 312
  tone-on-tone schemes 57
  white *258, 262–3, 278*
columns *117, 256–7, 265, 275, 290*
connection 262–5
Conran, Terence 31
Contardi *321*
contrast 41
corridors *54*
CTO Lighting *54*
curtain: texture *139, 153*
  see also drapes

D

Dahl-Wolfe, Louise *231, 314*
Danetti *278*
DARK *56–7, 211*
Davidts, Stéphane *212*
Day, Robin 27
daybeds *223*
De Castelli *248*
de Gournay *4, 108, 110*
Demo, Grillo *231*
desks *55, 101, 182*, 267, *267*
dining areas *64, 270, 273, 276–7, 281*, 282–93
  dark color schemes 165
  lighting *278, 279*, 282, *282–7*
  monochrome palettes *156*
  separating from living spaces *47–50, 55, 259, 277*
  use of accent colors in *182, 198*
displays: artwork 14, *24, 112, 132, 223, 232*, 245
  cabinets *177*
  everyday objects *16, 17, 18, 23, 41, 70, 227*
  flowers and plants *37, 43, 63, 148*
  star pieces *222–39, 261, 265*, 267, *274*
divans *40*
Dixon, Tom *67, 196, 213, 290–1, 284–5*
DK Home *218, 258, 277*
Dolron, Désirée *225*
door furniture 68, *70, 98, 100*
doors 95
  bespoke *96, 98, 99, 100*
  framing 68, *68–71*
  pivoting *206–7, 259, 290*
  sliding doors *70, 74–5, 110–11*, 262
Dornbracht *121, 304, 306*
double-height spaces *252–3, 256–7*
drapes *252–3*
  and accent colors *179, 189, 196*
  and grid lines 50
  textiles 144, *144, 145, 155*
dressing rooms *94, 97, 190*, 320–3
Duravit *304*

E

East-meets-West interiors 36–43, *319*
Edition Limitée *323*
Edwards, Guy 28, 29
Eicholtz *304*
Elle Decoration 26
entrance halls *45, 90, 201, 220, 242–7, 259*
Erro *105*

F

fabrics 138, 144–7, *169*, 193, 234, 310
faucets *121, 294*, 297, *299, 304, 307, 309*
feng shui 42, *122*, 238
fireplaces *58, 116, 141, 281*
Flanagan, Barry *293*
flooring 102–3
  wooden *94*, 102, *103, 155*
  see also runners
flow 46–77, 250
flowers and plants: as accent colors *182, 185, 189, 192, 196*, 197, *198*
  displaying *37, 43, 63, 148*
  scent and mood 234, *236–7, 238*, 312
  and texture 236
focal points 257
Fontana 224
Fontana Arte *276*
Fortuny *168, 244, 260*
frames *112, 117, 119*
framing 68–73
Fries, Pia *179*
functions 250
Fung, Spencer *313*
furniture *75*
  see also chairs; tables, *etc*
fusion 38–9

G

Galerie Negropontes *15, 242*
Galerie Van der Straeten *201*
Gallerie 16 *220*
gardens *25, 72–3*
Garouste & Bonetti *105*
Gervasoni *318*
Gessi *304*
Gibson, Ralph *52, 232*
Gill, David *6, 105, 193, 218*
gold 108–15
Goyal, Vikram and Divya *315*
Graham & Brown *166, 218, 304*
green accent colors 196–9, *237*
grids 46–77
  bathrooms *298*
  bedrooms *162–3*
  dining areas *288*
  displaying collections 231
  entrance halls *242*
  living areas 250, *256–7*, 257, 262
Guy, Christopher *117, 219*

H

Hadid, Zaha *6–7*
halls, entrance *45, 90, 201, 220, 242–7, 259*
hallways 102, *105*
handles 95
hats *18*
Hicks, David 31
Hive *271*
home offices *55*, 266–7
homework areas *270*, 271
Hoppen, Kelly: bar design *225*
  bathtub and faucet designs *294, 297, 299, 300–1, 302*
  chair designs *169, 196*
  coffee table designs *17*
  desk design *266*
  interlocking cubes *109, 309*
  island unit designs *279*
  lighting designs *180, 210, 211, 212*
  resin coral *238–9*
  rug designs *186*
  screen designs *134, 167, 174*
  shutter designs *92, 306*
  stool design *318*
  table designs *154, 157, 232*
  vase designs *195*
  wallpaper designs *166, 218, 304*
Horst, Horst P. *191, 313*
Hudson *12*
Hudson Furniture *115*
Hume, Kate *236*
Hunt, Holly *155, 261, 317*
Huynh, Jean Baptiste *270*

I

island units *279*

J

Jacobsen, Arne *320*
JNL Samara *62, 258*
joinery 94–101
  bespoke 52, *52–3, 76*
Jordan, Fiona *238*

K

Kander, Nadav *210, 323*
Kelly, Daniel *189, 201*
Kinon *76*
kitchens *117*, 268–93
  kitchen bars *280*
  lighting *278, 279*, 282, *282–7*
  storage *117*
  use of color in *180*, 282
Knoll *101, 192*
Kuo, Robert: copper-shelled snail *188*
  floor lamps *118, 154, 258, 262–3*
  stools *317*
  tables *12, 47, 134, 155, 201, 217*

L

L-shaped rooms *255*
La Fibule *179, 318*
Lahumière Design *233*
lamps *see* lighting
Langlais, Hervé *15, 242*
Lasvit *166*
Le Corbusier *266*
Lézard Électrique *204*
Liaigre, Christian: benches *184, 290–1, 312*
  chairs *115, 169, 189, 266, 267, 290–1, 293*
  daybeds *223*

INDEX

desks 267
lights 266, 313
sofas 47, 197, 258
stools 292
tables 37, 47, 112–13, 118, 186, 199, 227, 232, 254–5, 263
lighting 200–13
in bathrooms 294, 297, 300, 300–1, 304–8
in bedrooms 312, 312–13, 316, 318
ceiling lights 244
design 206–13
in dressing rooms 320, 321, 322, 323
effects of 132
in entrance halls 67, 201
floor lamps 47, 118, 130, 154, 193, 248, 255, 258, 261, 262–3, 317
Kelly Hoppen designs 180, 210, 211, 212
in kitchen and dining areas 208–9, 211, 212, 278, 279, 282, 282–7
lanterns 201, 246
in living areas 206–7
and mirrors 216, 217, 218
and mood 234
sparkling 204–5
and staircases 80–1, 84–8, 203, 213, 246
statement lighting 202, 204–5, 245–7, 262, 282, 312
table lamps 157, 195, 233
task lights 271
to define zones 262
wall lights 95, 97, 119, 212, 214
see also chandeliers; pendant lights
linen 144
living areas 118, 248–67
dividing open-plan 47–50, 55, 259, 277
lighting 206–7
neutral color schemes 154, 157
use of accent colors in 178, 180, 186, 199
Livra 304, 307
lobbies 67
Lupi, Antonio 307
Lustrerie, Mathieu 210

M
Magistretti, Vico 74
Mahdavi, India 135, 194, 225, 323
Martin, Andrew 134, 271
Massant 187
McMillan, Judith K 53
Medri, Davide 121
Megaron 120, 246
Melogranoblu 211
Meridiani 187, 317
metallics 104–25, 264
mezzanine areas 43
Miller, Dennis 186
Minottitalia 318
mirrors 214–21
in bathrooms 121, 297, 304
in bedrooms ...12, 215, 221, 318, 320
in living areas 55, 218–19, 221
in corridors and halls 54, 217, 220, 245
Missoni, Luca 183
Modénature 254, 267, 270, 273
Moissonnier 178, 182
Monpas 120
Monroe, Marilyn 15, 242, 254
mood 234, 257, 297, 300

N
Nahas, Nabil 6–7
niches 4, 76, 110, 117, 233, 265, 298, 307
nightstands 194, 317
Christian Liaigre designs 37, 47, 112–13, 118, 186, 199, 227, 232, 254–5, 263

O
objects, displaying 222–39, 265, 267
ocean colors 194–5
OCHRE 71, 88, 114, 119, 244, 273, 312, 313
Ogundehin, Michelle 26–31
Op De Beeck, Hans 74–5
open-plan spaces 250, 256–7, 257, 262

P
panels, glass 42
Parmentier, Stéphane 95
Pawson, John 30
pearl 124–5, 188
Pebble London 227
pendant lights: in bathrooms 107, 304
in bedrooms ... 71, 151, 160, 165, 166, 179, 312–13, 318, 321, 323
in dining areas 62, 257, 273, 284–8
in entrance halls and corridors ..15, 45, 54, 66, 67, 213, 242, 246
in living areas 56–7, 116, 122, 154, 206, 211, 252–3, 258
over staircases 82, 203, 213
see also chandeliers
photographs 12, 119, 232, 267
picture rails 50
pictures see artwork
pillows: accent colors 183, 185, 188, 192, 193
in bedrooms 158, 160–3, 165, 166, 167, 314
buttons on 125, 165, 167
textiles 145, 152, 152–3, 160, 161, 166, 167
pink 190–1
plants and flowers: as accent colors 182, 185, 189, 192, 196, 197, 198
displaying 37, 43, 63, 148
scent and mood 234, 236–7, 238, 312
and texture 236
Platner, Warren 192, 292
Poggenpohl 276
Polidori Barbera 61, 76, 316
Poliform 321
Porta Romana ..195, 214, 218, 317, 318
Pouenat 212
Promemoria 219, 244, 277, 317
Pucci, Ralph 318
purple 192–3
Putman, Andrée 318

Q
Quartermaine, Carolyn 198

R
red accent colors 186–9
Redler, Stuart 186
refrigerator 279
Reilly, Kevin 45, 82, 213, 270, 271
repetition 70
resin coral 238–9
Rhodes W1 58
Ritts, Herb 168
Romney, George 112
roof terraces 140
Rosberg, Keke 29
The Rug Company 182
rugs 37, 192, 235, 255, 266, 311
Kelly Hoppen designs 186
runners 58–67, 95
accent colors 188
in bathrooms 62, 64–7, 114, 296, 300–1, 303, 304, 307, 308
bed 34, 194, 314, 319
carpet 82, 83, 86
ceiling 55
in corridors and halls 45, 247
floor 45, 59, 61, 62, 69, 102, 245, 247, 278, 282–3
horizontal 56, 62, 64, 65, 67, 69, 247, 278, 282–3
Japanese style 15, 46
table 60
vertical 62, 63, 64, 74, 76, 101, 109, 114, 145, 151, 282–3
wall 59, 60, 61, 63, 64, 74, 76, 101, 109, 114, 151, 282, 312
window 254–5

S
St Paul Home 271
scents 234, 312
screens 120, 134, 262
antique 147
in bathrooms 308
Kelly Hoppen designs 167, 174
Sé 312, 313
senses 234–5
shades 137, 170–1
Shaw, Martin 29
shelving: bookshelves 133, 182
displaying art collections .226, 227
floating 50, 110, 151, 226, 227, 232, 298, 319
glass 132
and grids 50, 70, 75, 76, 77, 99, 101, 183
lighting 178
as room dividers 262
Zaha Hadid design 6–7
Shladovksy, Azadeh 20
Shoji, Miya 72–3
shoji screens 47, 51, 56, 70, 72–3, 74, 100
Shutterly Fabulous 306
shutters 55, 70, 90, 164, 170–1, 306
Siddeley, Randle 140
SieMatic 278
silver 116–23, 158
simplicity 42–3
sinks 298, 302, 304, 307, 309
Smallbone 279
sofas: Christian Liaigre designs ... 47, 197, 258
Promemoria design 244
textiles 144
Somerville, Amy 214
sound systems 234
Spina 84, 134, 160
spiritual objects 238–9
squares 74–7
Squint 174, 178, 184
staircases ...78–89, 135, 247, 259, 291
Arts and Craft 260
and color 184
lighting 80–1, 84–8, 203, 213, 246, 246
Stanwix, Matt 14, 245
star pieces 222–39, 261, 265, 267, 274
Starck, Philippe 31
steam rooms 305
Stefanidis, John 31
stools 187
Azadeh Shladovsky design 20
bar stools 278, 279
Bleu Nature design 169
Christian Liaigre design 292
Danetti design 278
India Mahdavi designs 225, 323
Kelly Hoppen designs 279, 318
La Fibule design 179
Spencer Fung design 313
vintage 147
storage 238
custom-made 52
dressing room 321–3
home offices 267
kitchen 117
structure 50–7
study 55, 266–7
Sub Zero 279
sulphur colors 178–81
Swarovski 86, 205, 246, 246
swimming pools 108, 110–11
symmetry 74, 95, 228, 257, 262, 265, 311, 321

T
tables: coffee 17, 20, 47, 62, 112–13, 154, 186, 258, 261
console 246
desks 55, 101, 182, 267, 267
dining 270, 271, 275, 276, 284–8, 290–1, 293
dressing 12, 313, 321, 322
Kelly Hoppen designs 17, 154, 157
Robert Kuo designs 12, 47, 134, 155, 201, 217
side tables 20, 47, 115, 119, 155, 260, 315
table settings 277
terraces 22
Terzani 247
textiles 144–7
texture 95, 124, 142–3
in bathrooms 118
in bedrooms 166, 170–1, 312–13, 318
and displays 231
Eastern interiors 41
fabrics 138
flowers and greenery 236
and light 132
neutral color schemes 148, 150, 152–63, 264
and senses 234
and use of accent colors 189
and walls 51, 100
tiles, mosaic 117
tone 264
Torfs, Anna 179, 186, 258
Toscoquattro 298
tradition 40–1
transparent materials 126–35, 143
Tuft, Diane 319
turquoise 195, 319

U
upholstery 176

V
Vanstone, Paul 1, 109, 291
vases: Anna Torfs designs ... 179, 258
Kelly Hoppen designs 195
vistas 257, 289
von Unwerth, Ellen 312

W
wall finishes: specialist plaster 76, 108–11, 114, 121, 133, 195, 242, 288, 307, 309, 316
timber panels 95, 151
wallpaper: Kelly Hoppen designs 166, 218, 304
textured 181
Waterfront 294
Wearstler, Kelly 31
Webster, Stephen 59, 131, 133, 137
Wedgwood 300
Wegner, Hans 21, 284–5
weightlessness 132–5
work surfaces 275
wow factor 257

Y
yellow accent colors 178–81

Z
zones 46–77, 250, 250–1, 262

ACKNOWLEDGMENTS

Every effort has been made to trace copyright holders of artworks, designs, and photography. We apologize in advance for any unintentional omissions and would be pleased to insert the appropriate acknowledgments in any subsequent publication.

Photography Credits
Page 1 Mel Yates ©; Page 4 Jacqui Small © (photographer: Mel Yates). Page 5 above left and below left Thomas Stewart ©; above right and below right Mel Yates ©. Pages 6–7 Jacqui Small © (photographer: Mel Yates). Pages 10–11 Nick Haddow ©. Page 12 Mel Yates ©. Page 15 Mel Yates ©. Page 16 Simon Upton/Interior Archive, Simon Upton/TIA Digital Ltd ©. Page 17 Jacqui Small © (photographer: Mel Yates). Page 18 Mike Toy © (www.miketoy.com). Page 19 Regal Homes ©. Page 20 Kelly Hoppen Interiors © (photographer: Steve Leung). Page 21 Jacqui Small © (photographer: Mel Yates). Page 22 Jacqui Small © (photographer: Vincent Knapp). Page 23 Jacqui Small © (photographer: Mel Yates). Page 24 Kelly Hoppen Interiors © (photographer: Steve Leung). Page 25 Jacqui Small © (photographer: Mel Yates). Page 34 Thomas Stewart ©. Page 37 Jacqui Small © (photographer: Mel Yates). Page 38 top left and top right Bill Batten ©; bottom left Simon Upton/ Interior Archive, Simon Upton/TIA Digital Ltd ©. Pages 39–41 Bill Batten ©. Page 42 top Bill Batten ©; bottom Jacqui Small © (photographer: Vincent Knapp). Page 43 Bill Batten ©. Page 45 Jacqui Small © (photographer: Mel Yates). Page 47 Jacqui Small © (photographer: Mel Yates). Pages 48–9 Mel Yates ©. Page 50 Yoo Lodha Estrella ©. Page 51 Jacqui Small © (photographer: Mel Yates). Page 52 Thomas Stewart ©. Page 53 top left Jacqui Small © (photographer: Mel Yates); top right and bottom right Jacqui Small © (photographer: Vincent Knapp); bottom left German Sheyn ©. Page 54 client's own ©. Page 55: top left Yoo Lodha Estrella ©; top right Kelly Hoppen Interiors © (photographer: Steve Leung); bottom left Jacqui Small © (photographer: Mel Yates). Page 56–7 Mel Yates ©. Page 58 Jacqui Small © (photographer: Mel Yates). Page 59 top left, bottom left and bottom right Jacqui Small © (photographer: Mel Yates); top right Thomas Stewart ©. Page 60 top left Jacqui Small © (photographer: Mel Yates); bottom left Thomas Stewart ©. Pages 60 right to 61 Mel Yates ©. Page 62 top left and top right Topwin Development Ltd ©; bottom left and bottom right Jacqui Small © (photographer: Mel Yates). Page 63 Jacqui Small © (photographer: Mel Yates). Page 64 top left Bill Batten ©; top right and bottom left Simon Upton/Interior Archive; Simon Upton/TIA Digital Ltd ©; bottom right Jacqui Small © (photographer: Mel Yates); Page 65 Jacqui Small © (photographer: Mel Yates). Page 66 top Mel Yates ©; bottom Jacqui Small © (photographer: Mel Yates). Page 67 top left Jacqui Small © (photographer: Vincent Knapp); top right client's own ©; bottom Jacqui Small © (photographer: Mel Yates). Page 68 Jacqui Small © (photographer: Mel Yates). Page 69 top left, top right and bottom left Jacqui Small © (photographer: Mel Yates); bottom right Jacqui Small © (photographer: Vincent Knapp). Page 70 top left, bottom left and bottom right Jacqui Small © (photographer: Mel Yates); top right Mel Yates ©. Page 71 Mel Yates ©. Pages 72–3 Jacqui Small © (photographer: Vincent Knapp). Page 74 left client's own ©. Pages 74 right to 75 left Jacqui Small © (photographer: Vincent Knapp); Page 75 right Jacqui Small © (photographer: Vincent Knapp). Page 76 top Jacqui Small © (photographer: Vincent Knapp); bottom left and bottom right Mel Yates ©. Page 77 Mel Yates ©. Page 79 Jacqui Small © (photographer: Mel Yates). Pages 80–1 client's own ©. Pages 82–3 Jacqui Small © (photographer: Mel Yates). Page 84 top left and bottom left Jacqui Small © (photographer: Mel Yates); bottom right Mel Yates ©. Page 85 Mel Yates ©. Page 86 top left, top center, top right, bottom left, and bottom center Jacqui Small © (photographer: Mel Yates); bottom right Jacqui Small © (photographer: Vincent Knapp). Page 87 top left Jacqui Small © (photographer: Vincent Knapp); bottom left, top right, and bottom right Mel Yates ©. Pages 88–9 Mel Yates ©. Page 90 Mel Yates ©. Pages 92–3 client's own ©. Page 94 top left Mel Yates ©; bottom left Kelly Hoppen Interiors © (photographer: Steve Leung); bottom right Jacqui Small © (photographer: Mel Yates); top right Topwin Development Ltd ©. Page 95 Topwin Development Ltd ©. Page 96 Kelly Hoppen Interiors © (photographer: Steve Leung). Page 97 client's own ©. Page 98 top left Topwin Development Ltd; bottom left and bottom right Jacqui Small © (photographer: Mel Yates). Page 99 top left and right Jacqui Small © (photographer: Vincent Knapp); bottom left Jacqui Small © (photographer: Mel Yates). Page 100 Jacqui Small © (photographer: Mel Yates). Page 101 Steve Leung, Kelly Hoppen Interiors. Page 102 top left Jacqui Small © (photographer: Mel Yates); top right Mel Yates ©; bottom right Jacqui Small © (photographer: Vincent Knapp). Page 103 Mel Yates ©. Page 105 Jacqui Small © (photographer: Vincent Knapp). Page 107 Mel Yates ©. Page 108 Jacqui Small © (photographer: Mel Yates). Page 109 Mel Yates ©. Page 110 left Kelly Hoppen Interiors © (photographer: Steve Leung). Page 110 right to 111 client's own ©. Pages 112 left to 113 right Mel Yates ©. Page 113 right Jacqui Small © (photographer: Mel Yates). Page 114 Jacqui Small © (photographer: Mel Yates). Page 115 Mel Yates ©. Pages 116–17 Jacqui Small © (photographer: Mel Yates). Pages 118–19 Mel Yates ©. Page 120 left Jacqui Small © (photographer: Mel Yates); right Jacqui Small © (photographer: Vincent Knapp). Page 121 left Jacqui Small © (photographer: Vincent Knapp); right Jacqui Small © (photographer: Mel Yates). Page 122 left Mel Yates ©; right Jacqui Small © (photographer: Vincent Knapp). Page 123 Jacqui Small © (photographer: Mel Yates). Page 124 left Topwin Development Ltd; right Jacqui Small © (photographer: Mel Yates). Page 125 left Thomas Stewart; right Jacqui Small © (photographer: Mel Yates). Page 126 Mel Yates ©. Page 129 Jacqui Small © (photographer: Mel Yates). Pages 130 left to 131 left Mel Yates ©. Page 131 right Jacqui Small © (photographer: Mel Yates). Page 132 Mel Yates ©. Page 133 Jacqui Small © (photographer: Mel Yates). Page 134 top left Jacqui Small © (photographer: Vincent Knapp); top right Mel Yates ©; bottom right Jacqui Small © (photographer: Mel Yates). Page 135 top left and bottom right Jacqui Small © (photographer: Vincent Knapp); bottom left Jacqui Small © (photographer: Mel Yates); top right Mel Yates ©. Page 137 Jacqui Small © (photographer: Mel Yates). Page 139 Bill Batten ©. Pages 140–1 Jacqui Small © (photographer: Vincent Knapp). Page 142 top left Thomas Stewart ©; top right Bill Batten ©; bottom right Mel Yates Jacqui Small ©. Page 143 top Thomas Stewart ©; bottom left Topwin Development Ltd ©; bottom right Mel Yates ©. Page 144 Jacqui Small © (photographer: Mel Yates). Page 145 top left and right Jacqui Small © (photographer: Vincent Knapp); bottom left Jacqui Small © (photographer: Mel Yates). Page 146 Jacqui Small © (photographer: Mel Yates). Page 147 left Jacqui Small © (photographer: Mel Yates); right Bill Batten ©. Page 148 Thomas Stewart ©. Page 151 Kelly Hoppen Interiors © (photographer: Steve Leung). Page 152 Jacqui Small © (photographer: Mel Yates). Page 153 top left and bottom right Jacqui Small © (photographer: Mel Yates); bottom left Thomas Stewart ©; top right Mel Yates ©. Pages 154–5 Mel Yates ©. Page 156 Thomas Stewart ©. Page 157 Kelly Hoppen Interiors © (photographer: Steve Leung). Page 158 Jacqui Small © (photographer: Mel Yates). Page 159 Mel Yates ©. Page 160 top left and top right Mel Yates ©; bottom left and bottom right Jacqui Small © (photographer: Mel Yates). Page 161 top left Mel Yates ©; top right Jacqui Small © (photographer: Mel Yates); bottom right Thomas Stewart ©. Pages 162–3 Mel Yates ©. Page 164 Mel Yates ©. Page 165 Jacqui Small © (photographer: Mel Yates). Page 166 top left, bottom left, and bottom right Jacqui Small © (photographer: Vincent Knapp); top right Yoo Lodha Estrella ©. Page 167 top left Thomas Stewart ©; top right and bottom left Jacqui Small © (photographer: Mel Yates). Page 168 Thomas Stewart ©. Page 169 top left and bottom right Jacqui Small © (photographer: Mel Yates); top right Jacqui Small © (photographer: Vincent Knapp). Pages 170–1 Jacqui Small © (photographer: Vincent Knapp). Page 174 Jacqui Small © (photographer: Vincent Knapp). Page 177 Jacqui Small © (photographer: Mel Yates). Page 178 top left Mel Yates ©; top right Jacqui Small © (photographer: Vincent Knapp); bottom left Jacqui Small © (photographer: Mel Yates); bottom right Mel Yates ©. Page 179 top left, center left, and bottom left Jacqui Small © (photographer: Vincent Knapp); top right Jacqui Small © (photographer: Mel Yates); bottom right Yoo Lodha Estrella ©. Page 180 top left Jacqui Small © (photographer: Vincent Knapp); top right, center right, and bottom right Bill Batten ©. Page 181 Yoo Lodha Estrella ©. Page 182 Mel Yates ©. Page 183 Jacqui Small © (photographer: Vincent Knapp). Page 184 top left, top right, and bottom right Jacqui Small © (photographer: Vincent Knapp); bottom left Jacqui Small © (photographer: Mel Yates). Page 185 top left Thomas Stewart ©; top right Andreas von Einseidel ©, bottom left and bottom right Jacqui Small © (photographer: Vincent Knapp). Page 186 top left, top right, and center left Jacqui Small © (photographer: Mel Yates); bottom left Yoo Lodha Estrella ©; bottom right Thomas Stewart ©. Page 187 top left, top center, and bottom right Jacqui Small © (photographer: Mel Yates); center left Topwin Development Ltd ©; bottom left and top right Mel Yates ©. Page 188 top left, top right, and bottom right Thomas Stewart ©; bottom left Topwin Development Ltd ©. Page 189 top left, bottom left, and bottom right Thomas Stewart ©; top right Jacqui Small © (photographer: Mel Yates). Page 190 top left, top right, and bottom right Mel Yates ©; bottom left Jacqui Small © (photographer: Vincent Knapp). Page 191 top left to bottom left Mel Yates ©; top right and bottom right Jacqui Small © (photographer: Mel Yates). Page 192 top left and bottom right Mel Yates ©; bottom left and top right Jacqui Small © (photographer: Mel Yates). Page 193 top left Bill Batten ©; center left, top right, and bottom right Jacqui Small © (photographer: Mel Yates); bottom left Jacqui Small © (photographer: Vincent Knapp). Page 194 top left, top right, and bottom right Mel Yates ©; bottom left Jacqui Small © (photographer: Vincent Knapp). Page 195 top left and bottom left Mel Yates ©; center left and bottom right Jacqui Small © (photographer: Vincent Knapp); top right Jacqui Small © (photographer: Mel Yates). Page 196 Jacqui Small © (photographer: Mel Yates). Page 197 top and center left Mel Yates ©; bottom left Thomas Stewart ©; bottom right Kelly Hoppen Interiors © (photographer: Steve Leung). Page 198 top left and top right Bill Batten ©; bottom left Mel Yates ©; bottom right Thomas Stewart ©. Page 199 top left Mel Yates ©; top right Jacqui Small © (photographer: Vincent Knapp); bottom Thomas Stewart ©. Page 201 Jacqui Small © (photographer: Mel Yates). Page 203 Jacqui Small © (photographer: Vincent Knapp). Pages 204–5 Jacqui Small © (photographer: Mel Yates). Pages 206–9 Mel Yates ©. Page 210 top left Jacqui Small © (photographer: Vincent Knapp); bottom left and bottom right Jacqui Small © (photographer: Mel Yates). Page 211 top left, top right, and bottom right Mel Yates ©; bottom left Jacqui Small © (photographer: Mel Yates). Page 212 top left Jacqui Small © (photographer: Vincent Knapp); top right German Sheyn ©; bottom left and bottom right Mel Yates ©. Page 213 top left Yoo Lodha Estrella ©; bottom left Mel Yates ©; bottom right Jacqui Small © (photographer: Mel Yates). Page 214 Mel Yates ©. Page 217 Jacqui Small © (photographer: Mel Yates). Page 218 top and bottom left Jacqui Small © (photographer: Mel Yates); bottom right Mel Yates ©. Page 219 top left Mel Yates ©; top right and bottom right Jacqui Small © (photographer: Mel Yates); bottom left Jacqui Small © (photographer: Vincent Knapp). Page 220 Mel Yates ©. Page 221 top Mel Yates ©; bottom left and bottom right Jacqui Small © (photographer: Mel Yates). Page 223 Jacqui Small © (photographer: Vincent Knapp). Page 225 Jacqui Small © (photographer: Vincent Knapp). Page 226 Mel Yates ©. Page 227 top left Jacqui Small © (photographer: Mel Yates), top right Kelly Hoppen Interiors © (photographer: Steve Leung); bottom right Jacqui Small © (photographer: Vincent Knapp). Page 228 top left Jacqui Small © (photographer: Mel Yates); bottom left Jacqui Small © (photographer: Vincent Knapp); bottom right Topwin Development Ltd. Page 229 top left and top right Thomas Stewart ©; bottom Jacqui Small © (photographer: Mel Yates). Page 230 Mel Yates ©. Page 231 top right and bottom right Jacqui Small © (photographer: Mel Yates); bottom left Thomas Stewart ©. Page 232 top left, center left, and top center Jacqui Small © (photographer: Mel Yates); bottom left Thomas Stewart ©; top right Nan Fung Developments ©; center right Pavel Jovik ©; bottom right Mel Yates ©. Page 133 top and bottom Jacqui Small © (photographer: Mel Yates); center Topwin Development Ltd. Page 235 Jacqui Small © (photographer: Vincent Knapp). Page 236 top left Topwin Development Ltd; top right and bottom right Thomas Stewart ©. Page 237 Thomas Stewart ©. Page 238 top left Jacqui Small © (photographer: Mel Yates); top right and bottom right Topwin Development Ltd ©. Page 239 right Kelly Hoppen Interiors © (photographer: Steve Leung). Page 242 Mel Yates ©. Page 244 Mel Yates ©. Page 245 Kelly Hoppen Interiors © (photographer: Steve Leung). Pages 246–7 Jacqui Small © (photographer: Mel Yates). Page 248 Mel Yates ©. Pages 250–1 Jacqui Small © (photographer: Vincent Knapp). Pages 252–3: Mel Yates ©. Pages 254–5 Jacqui Small © (photographer: Mel Yates). Pages 256–7 Mel Yates ©. Page 258 Topwin Development Ltd ©. Page 259 Jacqui Small © (photographer: Vincent Knapp). Page 260 Mel Yates ©. Page 261 Kelly Hoppen Interiors © (photographer: Steve Leung). Pages 262–5 Jacqui Small © (photographer: Mel Yates). Pages 266–7 Mel Yates ©. Pages 269–70 Jacqui Small © (photographer: Vincent Knapp). Page 271 Jacqui Small © (photographer: Mel Yates). Pages 272–3 Jacqui Small © (photographer: Vincent Knapp). Pages 274–5 Mel Yates ©. Page 276 Jacqui Small © (photographer: Mel Yates). Page 277 top Thomas Stewart ©; bottom Topwin Development Ltd. Page 278 Jacqui Small © (photographer: Mel Yates). Page 279 top left Jacqui Small © (photographer: Vincent Knapp); top right Mel Yates ©; bottom left Jacqui Small © (photographer: Mel Yates). Pages 280–1 Jacqui Small © (photographer: Mel Yates). Pages 282–3 Kelly Hoppen Interiors © (photographer: Steve Leung). Pages 284–5 Jacqui Small © (photographer: Mel Yates). Pages 286–7 Jacqui Small © (photographer: Vincent Knapp). Pages 288–93 Mel Yates ©. Page 294 Jacqui Small © (photographer: Mel Yates). Page 296 Jacqui Small © (photographer: Vincent Knapp). Page 297 Kelly Hoppen Interiors © (photographer: Steve Leung). Page 298 Jacqui Small © (photographer: Mel Yates). Page 299 top right and bottom left Jacqui Small © (photographer: Mel Yates); bottom right Mel Yates ©. Pages 300–1 Mel Yates ©. Page 302 Mel Yates ©. Page 303 top left, center left, and bottom left Jacqui Small © (photographer: Mel Yates); top right and bottom right Mel Yates ©. Page 304 top left Mel Yates ©; top right Jacqui Small © (photographer: Mel Yates); bottom Topwin Development Ltd ©. Page 305 Jacqui Small © (photographer: Mel Yates). Page 306 Mel Yates ©. Page 307 top left German Sheyn ©; top right and bottom right Mel Yates ©. Page 308 Shiamo ©. Page 309 top left Mel Yates ©; top right, Jacqui Small © (photographer: Vincent Knapp); bottom right Jacqui Small © (photographer: Mel Yates). Page 311 Jacqui Small © (photographer: Vincent Knapp). Pages 312–15 Mel Yates ©. Page 316 Jacqui Small © (photographer: Mel Yates). Page 317 Mel Yates ©. Page 318 top left Mike Toy © (www.miketoy.com); center left and top right Jacqui Small © (photographer: Vincent Knapp); bottom left and bottom right Mel Yates ©. Page 319 Kelly Hoppen Interiors © (photographer: Steve Leung). Page 320 Thomas Stewart ©. Page 321 Kelly Hoppen Interiors © (photographer: Steve Leung). Page 322 Jacqui Small © (photographer: Mel Yates). Page 323 Mel Yates ©.

Artist Credits
Page 1 sculpture by Paul Vanstone.
Pages 6–7 shelf by Zaha Hadid, "Dune 01," 2007, Editions David Gill, London; artwork by Nabil Nahas.
Page 15 *Portrait of Marilyn Monroe in a Black Dress*, c.1950, to promote *The Asphalt Jungle*, photograph by Ed Clark/The LIFE Picture Collection/Getty Images.
Page 16 photograph by Karl Blossfeldt © Karl Blossfeldt, Archiv Ann und Jürgen Wilde, Zülpich.
Page 47 artwork by Daniel Kelly of Kyoto, Japan, *Topsy Turvy* (2008), acrylic on Nepalese paper on wood panel.
Page 48–9 (left to right) photograph, *Ali Underwater* by Flip Schulke (Michael Hoppen Gallery); photograph by Duffy © Duffy Archive; photograph, *Brigitte Bardot* © Terry O'Neill/ courtesy of Richard Goodall Gallery; artwork by Ben Vautier; photographs, *Norma Shearer* by George Hurrell (Getty Images); *Steve McQueen* by William Claxton/courtesy Demont Photo Management; artwork by Kimiko Yoshida.
Page 50 artwork by Stuart Redler.
Page 52 photograph by Ralph Gibson (Michael Hoppen Gallery).
Page 53 top left bust, *La Fanciulla* by Ralph Brown; bottom right photographs by Judith K McMillan.
Page 57 top left artworks by Kimiko Yoshida.
Page 59 top right photograph, *Gary Cooper* by Cecil Beaton.

ACKNOWLEDGMENTS

Page 61 sculpture by Paul Vanstone.
Page 62 photographs by Simon Brown from the Kelly Hoppen range.
Page 66 top artwork by Kimiko Yoshida; sculpture by Paul Vanstone.
Page 74 right to 75 left *Determination (13)* (boy) and *Determination (2)* (girl), 2003, lightbox and photograph by Hans Op De Beeck/courtesy of the artist and Galerie Ron Mandos, Amsterdam.
Page 88 bottom left photographs by Ron van Dongen.
Page 90 *Portrait of Marilyn Monroe in a Black Dress*, c.1950, to promote *The Asphalt Jungle*, photograph by Ed Clark/The LIFE Picture Collection/Getty Images.
Page 105 artwork by Erro, © ADAGP, Paris and DACS, London 2016.
Page 109 right sculpture by Paul Vanstone.
Page 112 left painting, *Portrait of the Vernon Children* by George Romney.
Page 115 artwork, private collection (client's own).
Page 119 right photograph by Ron van Dongen.
Page 120 right metal sculpture by Megaron.
Page 135 top left artwork by Kimiko Yoshida.
Page 148 photographs by Ron van Dongen.
Pages 154 and 155 photographs by Ron van Dongen.
Page 156 photograph, *Accordionist, Esztergom, October 21, 1916*, by André Kertész.
Page 158 photograph by Ron van Dongen.
Page 165 top left artwork by Ben Vautier.
Page 168 photograph, *Glenn Close* (1994) by Herb Ritts/Trunk Archive.
Page 179 center left paintings by Pia Fries.
Page 183 artworks, *Moons* by Luca Missoni.
Page 184 top right artwork by Peter Beard.
Page 186 bottom left artwork by Stuart Redler.
Page 187 bottom left artwork by Ernst Haas, *Route 66 Albuquerque* (Getty Images).
Page 189 top right artwork by Daniel Kelly of Kyoto, Japan, *Topsy Turvy* (2008), acrylic on Nepalese paper on wood panel.
Page 190 top right photograph, *Kelly Hoppen* by David Bailey; photograph (right) by Louise Bobbe; bottom right antique-copper snail by Robert Kuo.
Page 191 second-from-bottom left photograph by Peter Beard; bottom left photograph, *The Mainbocher Corset* (1939) by Horst P Horst.
Page 193 bottom right photograph, *Central Park South* (1998) by Jason Langer.
Page 194 top right artwork by Neil Reddy.
Page 201 artwork by Daniel Kelly of Kyoto, Japan, *I Am Not a Geisha* (2006), lithograph, woodblock, hand-coloring on paper.
Page 207 bottom photograph by Duffy © Duffy Archive.
Pages 208–9 photograph by David Parker.
Page 210 bottom right photograph, *Jibby Beane* by Nadav Kander.
Page 211 top left artwork by Peter Beard; top right photograph, *Ali Underwater* by Flip Schulke (Michael Hoppen Gallery); photograph by Duffy © Duffy Archive.
Page 212 top left artwork by Peter Beard.
Page 223 artwork by Peter Beard (Michael Hoppen Gallery).
Page 225 photograph by Désirée Dolron, Grimm Gallery, Amsterdam.
Page 227 bottom right four West African bronze sculptures from Pebble London, www.pebblelondon.com.
Page 231 bottom left photograph by Louise Dahl-Wolfe/courtesy Staley-Wise Gallery, New York; bottom right sculptures by Grillo Demo from David Gill Gallery.
Page 232 bottom left photograph by Ralph Gibson (Michael Hoppen Gallery).
Page 238 top left Buddha from Fiona Jordan.
Page 242 *Portrait of Marilyn Monroe in a Black Dress*, c.1950, to promote *The Asphalt Jungle*, photograph by Ed Clark/The LIFE Picture Collection/Getty Images.
Page 244 photographs by Ron van Dongen.
Page 245 photographs, *From a Window of the Louvre* by Tom Artin (left); *A Bout de Souffle – Jean Seberg (Boulevard Saint-Germain)* by Raymond Cauchetier, Gelatin Silver Print, 1959 (James Hyman Gallery), www.raymond-cauchetier-photographs.com (right).
Page 250–1 *Portrait of Marilyn Monroe in a Black Dress*, c.1950, to promote *The Asphalt Jungle*, photograph by Ed Clark/The LIFE Picture Collection/Getty Images.; artwork by Kimiko Yoshido.
Page 254–5 *Portrait of Marilyn Monroe in a Black Dress*, c.1950, to promote *The Asphalt Jungle*, photograph by Ed Clark/The LIFE Picture Collection/Getty Images (left); *Jessica in Lace Dress* by Louise Bobbe from Stephanie Hoppen Gallery (far right).
Page 255 right artwork by Kimiko Yoshido; *Picasso with the Hat and Revolver of Gary Cooper* by André Villers, gelatin silver print, 1958; artwork by Ben Vautier.
Pages 256–7 artwork by Ben Vautier; photograph, *Norma Shearer* by George Hurrell (Getty Images).
Page 261 *Ablution* from 'The Barking Wall', 2010, by Brendan George Ko.
Page 266 artwork from the *Playboy* series by Julie Cockburn (left); photograph *Kings of Hollywood* by Slim Aarons (Getty Images) (center); photograph/artwork by Nobuyoshi Araki (Takaishii Gallery) (right).
Page 270 gelatine silver collection print by Jean Baptiste Huynh.
Page 290 top right photograph, *Ali Underwater* by Flip Schulke (Michael Hoppen Gallery); photograph by Duffy © Duffy Archive; photograph, *Brigitte Bardot* © Terry O'Neill/courtesy of Richard Goodall Gallery; bottom and page 191 sculpture by Paul Vanstone.
Page 293 bronze sculpture, *Hare* by Barry Flanagan.
Page 302 top left photograph, *Veronica Lake* by Eugene Robert Richee (Getty Images); bottom right photographs, *Audrey Hepburn Playing Golf*, Hulton Archive (Getty Images); *Patsy Pulitzer Leaning Against Seaplane* by Slim Aarons (Getty Images).
Page 312 photograph by Ellen von Unwerth/courtesy Staley-Wise Gallery, New York.
Page 313 photograph, *The Mainbocher Corset* (1939) by Horst P Horst.
Page 315 photograph by Louise Dahl-Wolfe/courtesy Staley-Wise Gallery, New York.
Page 319 artwork by Diane Tuft.
Page 320 photograph (left) by Ralph Gibson (Michael Hoppen Gallery).
Page 321 top right photograph by Csilla Szabo, *Streak 9*, Edition 1 of 7 (Saatchi Gallery).
Page 323 top photograph of Kelly Hoppen by David Bailey; photograph, *Jessica in Lace Dress* by Louise Bobbe from Stephanie Hoppen Gallery (left); photograph, *Jibby Beane* by Nadav Kander (bottom right).

Design Credits

Page 12 table by Robert Kuo, light by Hudson, bed by Promemoria.
Page 15 light by Hervé Langlais for Galerie Negropontes, bespoke table designed by Kelly Hoppen with bronze base by Matt Stanwix.
Page 17 coffee table by Kelly Hoppen.
Page 19 Oriental figurines from Asiatides.
Page 20 Torre stools by Azadeh Shladovsky.
Page 21 Wishbone chairs by Hans Wegner.
Page 25 stone sphere from Talisman.
Page 37 Flibuste pedestal tables by Christian Liaigre.
Page 45 pendant lights by Kevin Reilly.
Page 47 Augustin sofa, Gallet ottoman, L.N.A. cocktail table, and Chantecaille floor lamp by Christian Liaigre, Gobbi club chairs by Dennis Miller, Oval table by Robert Kuo.
Pages 48–9 Velin chairs and banquettes by Christian Liaigre, benches by Guillaume Alan, linear pendant light by Kelly Hoppen, Sera Lantern floor lamp (left) by Mark Brazier-Jones, Ribot lamp by DeCastelli (right).
Page 50 Gem Collection pendant lights by Tom Dixon, custom-made Munich table by Baltus, Diaz Due Chair by Meridiani, Dome Light by Aanngenaam XL, Large Swing Sconce by Jason Koharik, Newman sofa by Meridiani, Torre tables by Azadeh Shladovsky, vases by Anna Torfs.
Page 51 Augustin sofa, Chantecaille floor lamp, and Flibuste pedestal tables by Christian Liaigre, Gobbi club chairs by Dennis Miller.
Page 54 pendant light by CTO Lighting, sculpture by Arteriors.
Page 55 top left glass vase by Anna Torfs; top right Revolve table lamp by Bert Frank.
Pages 56–7 pendant light (foreground) by Kelly Hoppen with glass bubbles blown by DARK, pendant light (background) Hervé Langlais for Galerie Negropontes, Globe table lamp by Lee Broom, sofa and armchairs from the Kelly Hoppen Collection, Ribot floor lamp DeCastelli, Sera Lantern floor lamp Mark Brazier-Jones.
Page 58 top designed by Kelly Hoppen for Regal Homes, flowers by Sophie Eden; bottom chair by Jimmie Martin.
Page 59 bottom right ALMA leather floor.
Page 61 stools by Tom Dixon, Velin chairs by Christian Liaigre.
Page 62 top right Samara coffee table by JNL, Umberto side table by Christian Liaigre; bottom right Plaza armchair in white leather and Savoy lounge table by Modénature, Kolom pendant light by Kevin Reilly, silver tumblers by C Best.
Page 63 screen by Monpas.
Page 64 bottom left Series 7 chairs by Arne Jacobsen.
Page 67 top right perforated pendant light by Tom Dixon.
Page 69 top left Metropolis fire sculpture by BD Design; bottom right sofa by Andrée Putman (for Ralph Pucci), Swarovski crystal light, table by Robert Kuo.
Page 70 top left chairs custom-made by Talisman.
Page 71 pendant light by OCHRE.
Page 74 left Atollo table lamp by Vico Magistretti.
Page 77 shelf unit by Kelly Hoppen.
Pages 80–1 crystal chandelier by Robert Clift.
Page 82 lanterns by Kevin Reilly.
Page 83 lighting by Robert Clift.
Page 84 top left and bottom chandelier by Spina.
Page 85 top left and top right chandelier Dorian Caffot at Matthew Upham Antiques.
Page 86 top center and bottom center ottoman by Christopher Guy, console table by Megaron, Swarovski crystal light.
Page 87 bottom left chandeliers by Mark Brazier-Jones.
Pages 88–9 lighting cascade by OCHRE, wall lights by OCHRE, table from Moissonnier.
Page 90 pivoting shutters designed by Kelly Hoppen Interiors.
Pages 92–3 vase (foreground) by kellyhoppen.com.
Page 94 bottom left wall light by Stéphane Parmentier.
Page 95 wall lights by Glass and Glass Art.
Page 97 pendant lights by CTO Lighting.
Page 101 Platner chair for Knoll, pendant lights from Melogranoblu, Revolve table lamp by Bert Frank.
Page 105 chest of drawers by Garouste & Bonetti/courtesy of the David Gill Gallery.
Page 107 cut-crystal and brass pendants by Lee Broom.
Page 109 interlocking cubes of brass, mirror, and black anthracite by Kelly Hoppen Interiors, vintage Murano glass owl.
Pages 112 right to 113 left vases by Absolute Flower, coffee table by Christian Liaigre.
Page 113 vintage coffee table from Talisman, vintage Murano glass owl.
Page 114 light by OCHRE.
Page 115 Rock table by Hudson Furniture, armchair by Christian Liaigre.
Page 116 fire sculpture by BD Design, lighting by Robert Clift.
Page 117 right storage system by Kelly Hoppen for Smallbone.
Page 118 left floor lamp by Robert Kuo, Darder Wingback chair by Holly Hunt, side table by Christian Liaigre, White Flax pendant light by Jeremy Cole; right to 119 left bathtub by Agape, side table by Asiatides.
Page 119 right wall light by OCHRE.
Page 120 left screen by Monpas.
Page 121 left faucet by Dornbracht; right Bombato mirror by Davide Medri.
Page 122 left Fluid pendant lights by Beau McClellan.
Page 123 left Molten mirror by Christopher Guy.
Page 126 acrylic and wood blocks by Bleu Nature.
Page 129 vintage Bubble-style chairs by Kelly Hoppen Interiors, coffee tables by Kelly Hoppen, organic-shaped side table by Robert Kuo.
Page 130 left Sera Lantern by Mark Brazier-Jones; right to page 131 left bespoke chandelier by Mark Brazier-Jones.
Page 131 right Lord Carter chandelier by Mark Brazier-Jones.
Page 133 left Stephen Webster's flagship store in London, bespoke stool covered with skull-patterned snakeskin by ALMA Leather, lights by Mark Brazier-Jones.
Page 134 top left screen by Kelly Hoppen Interiors; top right crystal light by Spina, side table by Robert Kuo; bottom right table by St Paul Home, acrylic Saturn chairs Andrew Martin.
Page 135 top left Plexiglass Bubble chair by Eero Aarnio, floor lamp by India Mahdavi, Augustin sofa and Nagato stool by Christian Liaigre, Ring Screen by Kelly Hoppen; bottom left vintage Bubble-style chairs by Kelly Hoppen Interiors; bottom right glass Ghost chair by Cini Boeri for Fiam.
Page 140 wall of water by Randle Siddeley.
Page 143 bottom left vases from Chachkies.
Page 145 top left Opium chair by Christian Liaigre.
Page 146 banquettes by Kelly Hoppen.
Page 152 top left Velin banquette by Christian Liaigre; top right sink by Toscoquattro.
Page 153 bottom right frame chair by Baltus.
Pages 154 and 155 White Flax pendant light by Jeremy Cole, Darder Wingback chairs by Holly Hunt, floor lamps by Robert Kuo, sofas by Rose Uniacke, coffee table by Kelly Hoppen, Rock side table by Hudson, metal side table Christian Liaigre, custom-made circular table by Robert Kuo.
Page 156 tall wenge tables by Modénature.
Page 157 Globe table lamp by Lee Broom, side table by Kelly Hoppen Interiors.
Page 158 pendant light by Alison Berger from Holly Hunt, bench custom-made by Smith & Brown Cabinetmakers Ltd, vases Absolute Flowers.
Page 160 top left crystal wall light by Kelly Hoppen, reading light by Mr Light, chandeliers in gimbals by Arteinmotion; top right pendant light by Alison Berger from Holly Hunt; bottom right crystal chandeliers by Spina.
Pages 162–3 crystal wall light by Kelly Hoppen, reading light by Mr Light, chandeliers in gimbals by Arteinmotion.
Page 164 bedside lamps by OCHRE, pendant light by Tom Dixon, bed by Duxiana.
Page 165 bottom right Aloe Shoot ceramic pendant light by Jeremy Cole.
Page 166 top right Inhale pendant light by Lasvit Lighting, Square Panel 02-060 wallpaper by Kelly Hoppen for Graham & Brown.
Page 167 top right Ring Screen by Kelly Hoppen.
Page 168 Fortuny silk chair cover.
Page 169 top right chair by Kelly Hoppen, wooden stool by Bleu Nature; bottom right Aspre lounge chair by Christian Liaigre.
Pages 170–1 cylindrical glass pendant lights by Solzi Luce.
Page 174 Ring Screen by Kelly Hoppen, armchair by Squint.
Page 178 top right Ring Screen by Kelly Hoppen, armchair by Squint; bottom right cabinet by Moissonnier, table lamp by Porta Romana.
Page 179 center left sofa by Interior Craft, chair by Kelly Hoppen, vases by Anna Torfs, side tables by Bleu Nature; bottom left cylindrical glass pendant light Solzi Luce; bottom right TAO Pouf by La Fibule, 21.7 pendant lights by Bocci, nightstand, Cloonie side table 2001 and Bardot bed by Meridiani.
Page 181 21.7 pendant lights by Bocci, nightstand and Bardot bed by Meridiani, vase by C best.
Page 182 top right and bottom left chandelier by Beau McClellan, bookcase by Moissonnier, table by Bellavista, carver chairs by Munna, chairs by Holly Hunt, benches by St Paul Home, wall light by Promemoria; top left and bottom right kilim by The Rug Company.
Page 184 top right Velin banquettes by Christian Liaigre, lighting by Robert Clift; bottom left chairs by Squint, Bip Bip side tables by Promemoria, table lamps by OCHRE.
Page 186 top right and center left Gobbi swivel club chairs by Dennis Miller, Augustin sofas, Flibuste pedestal tables, and Chantecaille floor lamp by Christian Liaigre, floor lamp by Robert Kuo; bottom left XL Dome ceiling light Aanngenaam, large swing sconce wall lights by Jason Koharik, Newman sofa and Gong side table by Meridiani, Torre tables by Azadeh Shladovsky, vases by Anna Torfs, gold accessory by Objet de Curiostie; bottom right rug by Kelly Hoppen.
Page 187 top left ribbed silk rug by Rug Art with red embossed leather border by Moore & Giles; center left vases by Kelly Hoppen; bottom left and top right armchair by Massant in red leather from Garrett Leather, wall lamp from La Lampe Gras, side table by Holly Hunt, bed and nightstand by Meridiani; bottom right Belmondo armchairs and footstools by Meridiani, letter-shaped steel side tables by Andrew Martin.
Page 188 bottom left Sutra Throne chair by Mark Brazier-Jones.
Page 189 top right Velin chairs and Continent sideboard by Christian Liaigre; bottom right rug by Kelly Hoppen.
Page 190 top right stools by India Mahdavi, pendant lights from Edition Limitée.
Page 191 second-from-top left bowl of succulents by Atelier Vierkant and OneAbode; bottom left table by B&B Italia, chairs by Christian Liaigre, vase by Absolute Flowers; second-from-bottom left side tables from Sé.
Page 192 top left and bottom right Platner chair for Knoll, custom-made table by il laboratorio dell'imperfetto, stool by Christian Liaigre, bench custom-made by Doreen Scott, vase by Absolute Flowers, bowl by Kelly Hoppen; bottom left rug by Stark Carpet; top right light by OCHRE.
Page 193 top left studded wenge cabinet from David Gill Gallery; center left Liberty floor lamps from Estro; bottom right sofa by Meridiani, fabrics by Holly Hunt.

Page 194 top right armchair from Amy Somerville, pendant light from BHS, nightstand from Meridiani, Gervasoni bed from Letti & Co., mirrored Waterfall wall light by Porta Romana; bottom right table by India Mahdavi.
Page 195 top left and bottom left nightstand by kellyhoppen.com, table lamp and mirror by Porta Romana; center left lighting by Robert Clift; top right vases by kellyhoppen.com.
Page 196 top left Mirror Ball pendant light by Tom Dixon, Barcelona stool by Mies van der Rohe, nightstand from kellyhoppen.com, bed by Kelly Hoppen; bottom right chair by Kelly Hoppen.
Page 197 center left sofa by Christian Liaigre; bottom right bowl from Apparatus Studio.
Page 198 top right fabric by Carolyn Quartermaine; bottom left bespoke table designed by Kelly Hoppen with bronze base by Matt Stanwix; bottom right tables by Modénature.
Page 199 top left console tables by Christian Liaigre.
Page 201 Lustre Ovale lantern from Galerie Van der Straeten, table by Robert Kuo.
Page 204 Lézard Électrique wall light by Mathieu Lustrerie.
Page 205 Swarovski crystal light.
Pages 206–207 side table by Villiers (beside sofa), bronze Ajoure side table (bottom, far right) and Flibuste pedestal tables by Christian Liaigre.
Pages 208–9 Fluid pendant lights by Beau McClellan, table by Bellavista, chairs by Holly Hunt, benches from St Paul Home, carver chairs by Munna.
Page 210 top left Lalique-style floor lamp by Mathieu Lustrerie; bottom right Kelly Light Sculpture by Kelly Hoppen for Spina.
Page 211 top left White Flax pendant light by Jeremy Cole; bottom left hand-blown glass bubbles by Melogranoblu; top right bubble pendant lights (foreground) by Kelly Hoppen with glass blown by DARK, pendant lights by Hervé Langlais for Galerie Negropontes, bespoke table designed by Kelly Hoppen with bronze base by Matt Stanwix; bottom right chandeliers in gimbals by Arteinmotion, coffee tables by Oly Studio, armchairs by Kelly Hoppen Collection.
Page 212 top left bespoke lightboxes designed by Kelly Hoppen; top right Chinet wall sconces by Stéphane Davidts; bottom left bubble pendant lights by Kelly Hoppen with glass blown by DARK, bespoke linear pendant light designed by Kelly Hoppen, stools by Tom Dixon, Velin banquettes and chairs by Christian Liaigre, benches by Guillaume Alan; bottom right wall light by Tristan Auer for Pouenat.
Page 213 top left Gem pendant lights by Tom Dixon; bottom left wall lights and pendant lights by Kevin Reilly; bottom right bespoke lantern by Keven Reilly.
Page 214 Waterfall wall light by Porta Romana, armchair by Amy Somerville.
Page 217 table (reflected in mirror) by Robert Kuo.
Page 218 top mirror by DK Home, Saturn chair by Andrew Martin; bottom right Pioche mirror by Porta Romana, Botanic wallpaper by Kelly Hoppen for Graham & Brown.
Page 219 top left mirror by Christopher Guy, Aloe Blossom pendant light by Jeremy Cole, wall light Cinabre, coffee table by Kelly Hoppen, side table Promemoria; bottom left mirror from David Gill Gallery; bottom right mirror by DK Home.
Page 220 pivoting shutters designed by Kelly Hoppen, chair from Gallerie 16.
Page 221 bottom right reinterpretation of iconic Ball chair by Eero Aarnio.
Page 223 Saline daybed by Christian Liaigre, wooden vessel from Concho Bay.
Page 225 bar designed by Kelly Hoppen Interiors, stools by India Mahdavi
Page 227 bottom right console table and lamp by Christian Liaigre.
Page 229 bottom coffee table by Kelly Hoppen.
Page 230 custom-made cabinet by Smith & Brown Cabinetmakers Ltd.
Page 231 top right quartz section from Ganesh Retreats.
Page 232 center left bronze Ajoure side table by Christian Liaigre; top center chairs by Baltus, side table by Kelly Hoppen; top right Albedo table lamp by Lahumière Design; bottom right clay pots from Atelier Vierkant and planting by Phillo Flowers.
Page 236 bottom right vases by Kate Hume Glass.
Page 238 top right resin coral branches from kellyhoppen.com.
Page 239 right glass domes with resin coral from kellyhoppen.com.
Page 242 pivoting shutters designed by Kelly Hoppen, bespoke table designed by Kelly Hoppen with bronze base by Matt Stanwix, pendant lights by Hervé Langlais for Galerie Negropontes, chairs from Gallerie 16.
Page 244 sofa by Promemoria, ceiling lights by Fortuny Scheherazade, custom-made chandelier by OCHRE.
Page 246 console table by Megaron, oval ottoman by Christopher Guy, Swarovski crystal light.
Page 247 chainmail pendant light by Terzani.
Page 248 trio of pendant lights (background) by Hervé Langlais for Galerie Negropontes, bespoke table designed by Kelly Hoppen with bronze base by Matt Stanwix, glass bubble pendant lights (foreground) designed by Kelly Hoppen with glass blown by DARK, gold disk Ribot floor lamp by De Castelli, Globe table lamp by Lee Broom, sofa and armchairs from the Kelly Hoppen Collection.
Pages 250–1 dining table and white leather chairs by Modénature, chainmail pendant light by OCHRE, Perspex Bubble chair by Eero Aarnio, floor lamps by India Mahdavi, Augustin sofas and Nagato stool by Christian Liaigre, petrified wood stools by Bleu Nature.
Pages 252–3 chandeliers in gimbals by Arteinmotion, coffee tables by Oly Studio, armchairs by Kelly Hoppen, side tables by Sé, fireplace sculpture by BD Design, vases by Kelly Hoppen Ltd.
Pages 254–5 Ajoure side tables and Flibuste pedestal tables by Christian Liaigre, sofas by Modénature.
Page 255 right Sera Lantern floor lamp by Mark Brazier-Jones, Ajoure side table by Christian Liaigre.
Page 256–7 glass bubble pendant lights designed by Kelly Hoppen with glass blown by DARK, bespoke linear pendant light designed by Kelly Hoppen, gold disk Ribot floor lamp by De Castelli, Sera Lantern floor lamp by Mark Brazier-Jones, sofas and armchairs from the Kelly Hoppen Collection, Ajoure side table, Velin dining chairs, and banquettes by Christian Liaigre, benches by Guillaume Alan, stools by Tom Dixon.
Page 258 free-blown glass chandelier by Dale Chihuly, Augustin sofa and Tabou side table by Christian Liaigre, Samara coffee table by JNL, glass bowls by Anna Torfs, vase from Arcase Glass, ornaments from Objet des Curiosité, floor lamp and Dong Shan side table by Robert Kuo, large vases by DK Home.
Page 259 mirror by Davide Medri, glassware by Anna Torfs, floor lamp by David Gill.
Page 260 bronze side table by Asiatides, pillow from Fortuny.
Page 261 coffee tables by Casamilano, pendants and floor lamp by Holly Hunt.
Page 262–3 Galion console table by Christian Liaigre, metal-base floor lamps, round table with fluted base, and nest of side tables by Robert Kuo, figurative floor lamps by Porta Romana, vintage Bubble-style chairs by Kelly Hoppen Interiors.
Page 264 Galion console table by Christian Liaigre, metal-base floor lamps, round table with fluted base, and nest of side tables by Robert Kuo, bowls by Anna Torfs.
Page 265 metal-base floor lamps, nest of side tables, Copper Empire Drumstools (back left of top image), and coffee table (back right of top image) by Robert Kuo, figurative floor lamps by Porta Romana, vintage coffee tables by Kelly Hoppen (foreground), bowls by Anna Torfs.
Page 266 Cassina LC1 armchair by Le Corbusier, Barbuda armchairs and coffee table by Christian Liaigre, desk from kellyhoppen.com, floor lamp and pendant light by Kevin Reilly.
Page 267 desk and Spartane chair by Christian Liaigre, Ffe armchair by Modénature.
Page 269 stools by India Mahdavi.
Page 270 table by Modénature, pendant by Kevin Reilly.
Page 271 table from St Paul Home, Altar pendant light by Kevin Reilly, Saturn acrylic chairs by Andrew Martin, mirrors by DK Home, Hive pendant lights by Cravt Original.
Page 272–3 table and white leather chairs by Modénature, chainmail pendant light custom-made by OCHRE.
Page 275 pendant light designed by Kelly Hoppen.
Page 276 kitchen by Poggenpohl, Avico pendant light by Fontana Arte, ceramic vessels by Absolute Flowers.
Page 277 bottom pair of large vases (left) by DK Home, Libertine chandelier by Mark Brazier-Jones, Bassano Panca table and Roka chairs by Promemoria, black fishbowl Cyan vases on table by Chachkies.
Page 278 top kitchen by SieMatic, Patsy vases by DK home; bottom Mirage gas-lift stools by Danetti.
Page 279 top left refrigerator Sub-Zero; top right kitchen units and worktop by Kelly Hoppen for Smallbone, pendant lights by Light Years, bowls by Kelly Hoppen Ltd; bottom left chairs custom-made by Talisman.
Page 280 kitchen by Boffi.
Page 281 lighting by Robert Clift.
Page 282–3 accessories from Apparatus Studio.
Pages 284–5 Wing chairs by Tom Dixon, Wishbone dining chairs by Hans Wegner, pendant lights by Caravaggio.
Pages 288–9 chandeliers in gimbals by Arteinmotion, coffee tables by Oly Studio, armchairs by Kelly Hoppen, vases by Kelly Hoppen Ltd.
Pages 290–1 bespoke pendant light designed by Kelly Hoppen, Velin chairs, banquettes, and Ajoure side table by Christian Liaigre, benches by Guillaume Alan, stools by Tom Dixon, glass bubble pendant lights designed by Kelly Hoppen with glass blown by DARK, armchairs by Kelly Hoppen, Sera Lantern floor lamp by Mark Brazier-Jones, pivoting lacquered doors designed by Kelly Hoppen, sofa from the Kelly Hoppen Collection.
Pages 292–3 Platner chair for Knoll, round table custom made by il laboratorio dell'imperfetto, stool by Christian Liaigre, bench custom-made by Doreen Scott, vases by Absolute Flowers, bowl by Kelly Hoppen, kitchen cabinets by Boffi, oven, refrigerator, and appliances by Gaggenau, dining table by B&B Italia, dining chairs by Christian Liaigre, shutters by Shutterly Fabulous, doors custom-made by Smith & Brown Cabinetmakers Ltd.
Page 294 Starlet bathtub by Bette, KH2 faucets by Kelly Hoppen for Waterfront.
Page 297 Harmony bathtub by Kelly Hoppen for Apaiser.
Page 298 bottom right sink by Agape, faucet by Waterfront, shutters by Kelly Hoppen, Quadrato towel radiator by Bisque, vase C Best; top right sink and block faucet from Toscoquattro.
Page 299 top right faucets designed by Kelly Hoppen, lighting designed by Robert Clift and Kelly Hoppen; bottom left cut-out sink by Toscoquattro.
Pages 300–1 Harmony bathtub by Kelly Hoppen for Apaiser; Patera light sculpture by Niamh Barry.
Pages 302 top right and bottom left Origami sink and bathtub by Kelly Hoppen for Apaiser, side table from Sé.
Page 303 top left ceramic sinks by Rifra; bottom right bathtub CP Hart, faucets Dornbracht, side table by Pols Potten.
Page 304 top left Botanic wallpaper by Kelly Hoppen for Graham & Brown, faucet by Dornbracht, pendant lights by Eicholtz; top right faucet by Gessi with controls by Kelly Hoppen for Waterfront; bottom Duravit Daro bathtub, Mem faucets from Dornbracht, Wavy Willow marble from Livra, vases from Chachkies.
Page 306 top and bottom left shutters by Kelly Hoppen for Shutterly Fabulous, Eramosa stone walls and sink from Limestone Gallery, faucet and shower by Dornbracht, bidet by Antonio Lupi; bottom right wall paneling by Barn in the City, shower fixtures by Dornbracht.
Page 307 top left designed by Kelly Hoppen with Yoo, sink by Boffi Spa, faucet by Waterfront, Zig Zag Flower stool Pols Potten; top right Jura gray honed limestone from Livra; bottom right sink by Apaiser, faucet by Antonio Lupi.
Page 309 top left interlocking boxes of brass, mirror, and black anthracite by Kelly Hoppen Interiors, vintage Murano glass owl.
Pages 312–13 glass pendant lights by OCHRE, damask bench and table lamp by Christian Liaigre, dressing table and stool by Spencer Fung, mirror by Rue de Lilles Paris, side tables from Sé.
Pages 314–15 glass pendant lights by OCHRE, damask bench by Christian Liaigre, chaise longue by Kelly Hoppen for kellyhoppen.com, throw from Hermès, metal table by Vikram and Divya Goyal.
Page 317 Frou Frou bed by Promemoria, Lennox nightstands by Holly Hunt, Keaton sofa and small armchairs by Meridiani, Copper Empire Drumstool by Robert Kuo, floor lamp and GLB 63 Droplet table lamps by Porta Romana, ottoman custom-made by Thomson Schultz in leather by Holly Hunt.
Page 318 top left nightstands and stool by Kelly Hoppen, pendant lamps Gervasoni, armchair by La Fibule, mirrors by Minottitalia; center left sofa Andrée Putman (for Ralph Pucci); bottom left and bottom right white ceramic Aloe Shoot pendant lights by Jeremy Cole, linen bench by Porta Romana.
Page 320 Swan chair by Arne Jacobsen.
Page 321 top left pendant lights by Contardi; top right accessories from kellyhoppen.com; bottom right storage units by Poliform.
Page 323 stools by India Mahdavi, pendant lights from Edition Limitée.

Author's Acknowledgments

Firstly, I would like to start by acknowledging my clients, as well as my friends, who have continued to have faith in my creations throughout my 40-year career, and who have allowed me to come back into their homes to photograph them time and time again.

To the companies and organizations that allow me to exhibit their work. Our collaborations have been nothing but a joy. Without your backing, none of this would have been possible.

To the journalists and authors, for always echoing my true style and intentions through their writing.

To the photographers who continue to capture my work and translate my vision with great ease. The amazing photographs within this publication, and those in previous books, are testament to all of your real talents. Thank you.

A huge thank you must also go to all the people who play a key role in my incredible team, who contribute in any way to bringing my vision to life and provide a constant charge of creativity. This, in particular, goes to my incredible team of interior designers, who execute every task with such precision and design expertise, as well as continuing to provide me with endless day-to-day support. The success that has resulted is a reflection of all of your genuine hard work and incredible design, and for that I will be forever indebted.

To all those experts who have helped me in the craftsmanship of my soft furnishings, who seamlessly realize my ideas, and the professional lighting designers who devise all the lighting schemes that enhance my work so brilliantly. Thank you also to the flower and garden designers, for providing such flair, design, and art to complement the Kelly Hoppen brand.

To the building companies that have constructed all of the properties that showcase my work in such a beautiful manner, and to the builders themselves, who have worked tirelessly.

To my PR family, who are integral to my success. Thank you for helping me to obtain the exposure that has made the Kelly Hoppen enterprise what it is today. Every task is carried out to absolute perfection.

To my extended team of publishers, stylists, researchers, accountants, PAs, and assistants. All of your contributions have allowed me to continue with my design of beautiful interiors. You have provided me with constant assistance and your network of support can be deemed as nothing but pure professionalism.

And last, but by no means least, to my amazing family. Day in, day out, you are there for me and I thank you all from the bottom of my heart.

Publisher's Acknowledgments

Jacqui Small would like to thank Kelly Hoppen for all her time and creative input in selecting images and making the book look and feel so beautiful.

Many thanks to the team at Kelly Hoppen Interiors for all their help, especially Christina Failutti, Lucy Humphries, Lee McNichol, Rhys Meggs, and Alexandra Bennaim. Thanks also to Michael Hoppen and his team at the Michael Hoppen Gallery.

Sincere thanks to all the talented photographers who have provided such stunning imagery for the book: Mel Yates, Vincent Knapp, Thomas Stewart, Bill Batten, Simon Upton, Steve Leung, Mike Toy, German Sheyn, Andreas von Einseidel, Paval Jovik, and Nick Haddow. Thanks also to Topwin Development Ltd, Yoo Lodha Estrella, and Nan Fung Developments.

Thank you to Sir Terence Conran for writing the Foreword, and Michelle Ogundehin for interviewing Kelly for the Q&A.

A big thank you to the team who helped put this book together: Eszter Karpati, who meticulously oversaw all aspects of the project from beginning to end, Robin Rout, Joe Hallsworth, and Zia Mattocks, who also wrote and edited the text.